To Pay the Piper
Federal Default Inevitable

by

Walter J. Lander

authorHOUSE

1663 LIBERTY DRIVE, SUITE 200
BLOOMINGTON, INDIANA 47403
(800) 839-8640
www.authorhouse.com

First published by AuthorHouse 08/13/04

ISBN: 1-4184-2223-1 (e)
ISBN: 1-4184-2222-3 (sc)

Library of Congress Control Number: 2004093155

Printed in the United States of America
Bloomington, Indiana

This book is printed on acid-free paper.

INTRODUCTION

The disaster on September 11, 2001, was a painful awakening for the American people and for the United States government to the continuing malignant existence of the al-Qaeda. This worldwide terrorism organization has been around and growing over a long period of time. September 11 was not the first notice of its destructive power. The one tower of the World Trade Center was bombed with a car bomb (1993), the U.S. barracks in Saudi Arabia was bombed with a car bomb (1995-96), U.S. embassies in East Africa were bombed with car bombs (1998), and the USS Cole was bombed with a boat bomb.(2000)

Suppose that Mr. Clinton, the then president of the United States at the time of any one of these earlier bombings, had decided to engage in a war to rout the Taliban for harboring the al-Qaeda. Could he have succeeded in persuading the nation to do it? Probably not. There would have had to be some kind of a national crisis similar to September 11 to warrant a reaction of war magnitude. The consequences of none of the earlier attacks were drastic enough. It took a devastating sneak attack on Pearl Harbor before the government could bring the nation to enter World War II. It took the devastation of World War II and the total prostration of Japan before the Japanese government and people were motivated to improve the quality of their products, reduce the costs, and emerge as a world industrial power. Had the single World Trade Center tower collapsed in the 1993 bombing, wreaking havoc on a large area of the city and with a much greater loss of life, Mr. Clinton might then have been able to lead the country to war. Without such major crises, people are prone to do nothing. Why is that?

First, it is difficult to comprehend the potential danger of not taking action in such circumstances. People are very much like the story of the frog. It is said that, if a frog is dropped into a pan of hot water, it will promptly jump out, but if a frog is placed in a pan of cool water and the pan set over a fire, the frog will sit there until the water boils and the frog is cooked. The water heats up too slowly for the frog to notice the rising temperature. There may be truth to this story because most humans react much the same way.

The second reason is that people are loath for action to be taken which would change the status quo. Although change is inevitable for all of us and occurs with some regularity, we do not like it, because adapting to it is stressful and sometimes even traumatic. We become comfortable with the way things are. While we may not particularly like things the way they are and recognize that they may get worse if nothing is done, we are still reluctant to do anything. How many times have we heard the old saws, "Don't rock the boat?"or "Better the devil we know than a devil we don't know."

The third reason is that action, whether it is reaction or pro-action, is expensive. Pro-action is easily the more expensive because the supposed need for it may never materialize. The money has been spent and wasted for nothing. Because we are loath to take action, governments are prone to tinker at the edges of problems by trying (often without success) solutions tried before in slightly different forms. Such solutions usually are the least radical and also the least effective. Sometimes we devise symbolically, "feel good" solutions that have no chance of success at all, such as tying a yellow ribbon around a tree if you wanted the Americans taken prisoners by the Iranians in 1979 to be freed.

The federal government appears to be dealing with terrorism now in an effective way. It would have been much better if the government had correctly perceived the danger ahead of time and had dealt with it pro-actively when increased intelligence efforts, an enforceable immigration law, and a stronger Immigration and Naturalization Service might have handled the problem more easily, with less cost, and without the staggering loss of life that occurred on September 11.

The United States has grown to become a great nation. There are two situations facing the United States right now which represent threats to the viability of the United States as a great nation, possibly greater than does al-Qaeda. They are related. One is overpopulation and the other is a large and growing cost of the federal government which already hangs like a millstone around the neck of the United States economy. These situations, like terrorism before September 11, are receiving scant attention and are not likely to receive more, absent some form of intervention, until they rise up to bite us in the future.

Overpopulation, in terms of simply too many people, is not so much a problem for the United States as it is for some other countries in the world, but here we have a variant of the overpopulation problem – a drastically low ratio of producers to eaters or P/E Ratio and a ratio sure to become lower in years to come as the baby boomers begin to retire. Economists project demographic data ten or twenty years into the future and see the producer/eater ratio deteriorating even further than it is today. The burden on producers in trying to support both themselves and the eaters will become intolerable. For many, it is intolerable now. The government has always sought to provide for the eaters, but without attempting to restrict their number or to increase the number of producers. Restricting the growing number of eaters and increasing the number of producers is something that must be done to resolve this problem. There are ways to do this, but how it should be done will be controversial.

There are also ways to reduce the cost of government and improve the extent to which it actually represents the people. The trick, in both cases, will be in finding ways of accomplishing these ends that are the least painful, most effective, and the most acceptable to society. Left alone, it is inevitable that the size and cost of government will continue to grow. Here's why. The Greeks discovered a couple of thousand years ago that elected officials could use tax money to buy votes. What elected officials do is to use tax money in various ways to benefit their own constituents, campaign contributors and potential contributors, although such expenditures may not be for the good of the electorate as a whole. They do this in the often-justified hope of winning more votes for themselves. This has been the practice for years in some democracies elsewhere in the world, but in the United States, it did not really begin to blossom until the 1930s with President Franklin D. Roosevelt's cynical policy of tax, tax, spend, spend and elect, elect.

This practice is often humorously expressed as, "He who robs Peter to pay Paul can always count on the vote of Paul." Some politicians have made a career out of this practice. By vigorously pursuing benefits and subsidies for their own constituents and special industries who are (and those who plausibly represent that they are) poor, disadvantaged, disabled, handicapped, discriminated against or incapacitated, these politicians have built powerful constituencies for themselves. They use other people's money collected by the government as taxes to do their personal good works. In the process, they have fostered dependencies of various classes of individuals and whole industries, and made comfortable livings for themselves in the process.

In this process, elected officials, political appointees, and career employees of the government conjure up more and more ways that government can benefit campaign contributors and their own constituents. In each case, a new program (or programs) is concocted, laws are enacted, regulations are written (or rewritten), funds are appropriated, new personnel are hired, and either taxes or indebtedness is increased. These programs take many forms, including: guaranteed prices, protective tariffs, production or import quotas, outright gifts, insurance of various kinds on favorable terms, set minimum wages, living wages, aid to families with dependent children, rent subsidies, school lunch programs – and the list goes on. In each case, the recipients tend to become dependent. They often become eaters because, with the subsidy, they are not forced to hustle and so begin to consume more than they produce, if they produce anything at all.

The primary and overriding objective of elected officials is getting reelected. It may happen at times to be in agreement with other objectives that are beneficial to the nation as a whole, but if so, it is coincidental. New candidates running for office often have noble and lofty goals. Once elected, however, they usually undergo a metamorphosis, and everything becomes subordinated to their own need to get themselves reelected. Sam Rayburn, a former speaker of the House of Representatives, is credited with the statement that, "Politics is the art of the possible." Actually, politics has become "the practice of self-interest." They become *career* politicians, an occupation that is usually better than anything they ever experienced before and better than anything they could go back to if defeated for reelection. These career politician jobs sometimes take on the attributes of a dynasty. The father's elected position, when he dies, can be passed on to one of his children or to his wife. Here is what Abraham Lincoln said about politicians:

Politicians [are] a set of men who have interests aside from the interests of the people, and who, to say the most of them, are, taken as a mass, at least one long step removed from honest men. I say this with the greater freedom because, being a politician myself, none can take it personally.

Greatly improved communications and television in particular has enabled us to see politicians for what they really are. However, we should not be too critical of them, because it is the electoral system that causes them to do what they do.

If these statements are true, one may well ask why it is that nothing has been done so far to either improve the producer/eater ratio or to reduce the size and cost of government. There are several reasons beyond the three listed above.

The first reason is that the people in the United States suffer a national addiction to government. It would be hard to find anyone – even the most common man or woman in the street – who is not in some way benefitted in a personal way by government which has slowly insinuated itself deeper into all of our lives over the last 60 or 70 years. Although individual citizens and taxpayers such as barbers, construction workers or shopkeepers are not favored with direct subsidies (as are members of many political blocs and pressure groups), they may have an aged parent in a nursing home whose stay there is funded by Medicaid. The student may have a government loan or a government-backed loan. The mother may be benefitted by government subsidies to child daycare facilities. Like children who have been given a piece of candy, once the government has bestowed a benefit on us as adults, we will not relinquish it easily. We all seem to feel that there is a giant government cornucopia somewhere in the sky, and if we can just push the right buttons, it will rain down on us all kinds of goodies. It will not happen. The government does not have any money except what it takes from us in taxes, and the amount that it gives back to the ordinary taxpayer is only the crumbs. That is the way it is.

A second reason that significant changes in these areas have not been made already is because there has been no identified group able and willing to do it. The career politicians of today will not do it because they are among the largest benefactors of big government. In fact, they will vigorously resist it, and who could blame them? They have prestigious jobs, good pay, and unparalleled benefits. They are wined and dined and lionized everywhere they go. How about the military? No way. High-ranking military leaders also have cushy jobs and are not disposed to disrupt the status quo. How about paramilitary groups like the Freemen, the Militia, the Posse Comitatis, and white supremacy groups? Not a chance. The Federal Bureau of Investigation, the Internal Revenue Service, the Drug Enforcement Administration, and the Bureau of Alcohol, Tobacco and Firearms will see to that. How about our business leaders? Not likely. Big business likes the corporate welfare it receives from government and finds big government easy to deal with. Could an independent party such as the Libertarian Party, the Green Party or the Reform Party do it? Improbable. These parties try to play the same game as the two major political parties in the United States but are at a tremendous disadvantage because of their small size and funding. However, any one or all of them, if they wished to do so, might in some way facilitate the implementation of the Grass Roots Empowered Electoral System outlined in Part III below.

One group should do it and surely can do it. That group is the common people, the typical empowered American taxpayer. We are adults. We work. We are educated. We pay taxes, vote, get married, and have children. We abide by the law to the extent that we know it and lead moral lives. We are the stuff this nation is made of. We produce the wealth of the nation. *We* can do it. *We* have the power. The change must start at the bottom, with the typical empowered American taxpayer; that is, with you and me. Otherwise, no material change will ever be made. But, is it within the realm of possibility for ordinary people to effect such changes? It is. This book suggests the way it can be done within both the law and the system.

Our founding fathers recognized that we have the right to do it. Here is what the Declaration of Independence says:

We hold these Truths to be self-evident that ... Governments are instituted among Men, deriving their just Powers from the Consent of the Governed, that whenever any Form of Government becomes destructive of these Ends, it is the Right of the People to alter or abolish it, and to institute new Governments, laying its Foundation on such Principles and organizing its Powers in such Form, as to them shall seem most likely to effect their Safety and Happiness.

This is what the Preamble to the United States Constitution says:

We, the People of the United States, in Order to form a more perfect Union, establish Justice, insure domestic Tranquility, provide for the common defence (sic), promote the general Welfare, and secure the Blessings of Liberty to ourselves and our Posterity, do ordain and establish this Constitution for the United States of America.

Our forefathers had the right, and we certainly have the right because nothing in that regard has changed. What is needed is a way to do it legally and peacefully. Can we do it by waving our homemade banners, shouting, and demonstrating in the streets? Not likely. Will writing to our governmental representatives do it? Not a chance. But, because we have the vote and because we live in a nation with a tradition of democracy, we have the ultimate power to revoke as much of the authority that we have given up to government as we wish and to exercise a greater degree of control over our own lives.

A third reason needed changes have not already been made are the unreasoned beliefs and attitudes that we carry with us from childhood. Almost from the moment a child is born, he begins accumulating information in his brain very much like a computer may accumulate information over a period of time in a data bank. At first, the child is absorbed with satisfying his own physical and psychological needs, with learning to manipulate his own body, and with learning about his environment. Later, the child accumulates information by the spoken word and example of his parents (unfortunately not always in agreement). The child is taught to say his prayers, is urged to eat his vegetables, and to not play with his food. Later, when the child has become toilet trained, he is taught to always flush. Outside, at first, he is taught not to venture out onto the street; later, to always hold the hand of his parent when crossing the street and, still later, to always look both ways before crossing.

Still later, the child starts into secular pre-kindergarten, kindergarten, or grade school and may begin attending a religious catechism or Sunday school class. The volume of information in the child's memory continues to grow, and this goes on for a lifetime. Unfortunately, some of the information absorbed by the child is incorrect either because the information presented was incorrect to start with or – even when the information presented was correct – the child incorrectly perceived it. Either way, some incorrect information finds its way into memory, and all of the information in memory – both correct and incorrect – taken together forms the basis for a person's attitudes which, in turn, shape all the decisions a person makes in his life.

Once the information is included in memory, it is rarely reviewed for accuracy, remains there correct or not, and continues to affect the person's attitudes and decisions. Exhuming unconscious conflicts or early-life traumas buried in memory may be an expensive and time-consuming process requiring the assistance of a skilled psychologist. Fortunately, one should be able to thoughtfully and objectively review one's attitudes without trying to piece together the various pieces of information in memory that resulted in their formation. People need to do this.

If you are reading this and live in the United States, the chances are overwhelming that you are a Christian. Moreover, you are of a particular sect within the Christian religion. Why is that? Usually, it is not because you consciously chose this religion and this sect; it is because your parents were of this religion and this sect, and they selected it for you. You had little to say about the selection at the time, and have since given little conscious thought to it yourself. If you were an East Indian living in India, you would probably be a Hindu and believe that Hinduism was the one and only religion. We were taught about religion and many other things by our parents, teachers, clergy, and friends when we were very young and did not have the mental capacity to objectively evaluate them. When we were grown and had the capacity, most of us never had either the time or inclination. Nobody deprecates this tendency, of course. It is necessary. If we did not accept what our parents and teachers tell us, we would have to reason out or experiment by trial and error with everything. Civilization would not have progressed far beyond the Stone Age. Although accepting is necessary, we have to sometimes examine critically some of these things we have accepted because conditions and circumstances change and, if we do not examine them occasionally, we will wind up slavishly doing some foolish things.

What is true of religion is true of other things, including government. More than 200 years have elapsed since this nation was founded and, despite significant changes in our customs and incredible technological developments, there have been surprisingly few changes in our political structures, institutions and practices. We believe that the national Constitution and the Bill of Rights are practically sacrosanct although they have changed little in 200 years. That is what we have been taught. It does not matter that conditions and circumstances are far different today than they were 200 years ago when they were created. At that time, it took four days on a fast horse to travel from Philadelphia to New York. Then, there was no radio, television, telephone, fax, e-mail, air, rail, or automobile travel. Our founding fathers did the best they could at the time, and they did well. Nevertheless, if they were doing it again today, would they do the same thing in all respects for a nation that now numbers 50 states and 290 million people? Probably not.

Many of our laws reflect attitudes that we acquired in the same way. For example, nearly everyone believes that suicide and prostitution are wrong (immoral). That is evident because most jurisdictions have laws that prohibit these actions and punish those who engage in either of them. We need to consider logically <u>why</u> these and other things are considered to be wrong – or right. Maybe they are not anymore, at least in some circumstances. The point is that it is difficult for people to opt for changing something, even if it is something about which they have given critical thought. John Maynard Keynes once said that the difficulty lies not in the new ideas but in escaping from the old ones.

We are a nation constituted as few other nations have ever been constituted before, of a mélange of peoples of many races, ethnic groups, religions, colors, and national origins. This is a book for those of us who regard the population, not as blacks or whites, not as Orientals or as Occidentals, not as Christians, Jews, or Muslims, not as Europeans, and not as Native Americans or Latinos, but as Americans. Although we are widely diverse in our backgrounds, religions, and cultures, our own futures are bound together in the future of this nation. All of us and the nation as a whole will benefit the most if we can put aside our personal and factional interests and act together for the common good. We hope, of course, that such will be the eventual course of events, but there is no assurance that it will.

This book suggests that we reconsider many attitudes and beliefs we have held for years but have never really thought much about, and further suggests that each of us use reason and logic as best we can to come to right conclusions about better ways to do things and then act on those conclusions. The suggested solutions to problems in most cases are radically different from the kinds to which we have become accustomed, and many people will be aghast at their unconventionality. It is true that some of the suggested solutions would require changes in federal and state constitutions and laws before they could be implemented. If these solutions are not acceptable now, there will come a time when radically different solutions such as those suggested will be viewed through a different lens out of absolute necessity. That time will be when the federal government can no longer fulfill the many obligations it has taken on. It will happen as described in Part I. Solutions scorned today may be quite acceptable then. One must recognize that many truths today were once heresy. Because timeworn solutions to these problems have been tried over and over again without notable success, new and (what will look like) radical solutions are required.

Many columnists, editors, news writers, commentators, politicians, and pundits correctly perceive the nation's economic, social, and governmental problems. They write and speak about them as well, but perhaps you have noticed that few of them have much to suggest about ways for significantly improving our situation. Why is that? It is because solutions other than mere tinkering are considered politically unfeasible. Indeed, many *are* unfeasible in today's social and political environment because career politicians will not support any but the most mundane solutions for fear of ridicule by the media which might, in turn, lead to their losing the next elections.

This book is replete with thoughts about what to do and how to do it. Some of the ideas propounded can be implemented at this time. Others cannot and must await the proper economic, political, and social climate, but I have set them out, nonetheless, so that when the time does come – as it surely will – they will be available for anyone who believes they have merit. If nothing else, I hope they will inspire the commencement of some fresh thinking in these areas by others. The obstacles to making the changes are admittedly colossal, but the task is not impossible. It requires merely a widespread effort by ordinary people with focus and perseverance. IBM's one-word motto is THINK. We must both think *and* do.

In trying to think through solutions to the problems described above, one should avoid imposing unnecessary conditions or requirements on the solution. For example, a little puzzle often given to students in business management courses is to mark on paper three rows of three dots each, one row above the other, forming a square or a block of nine dots. The challenge is to connect all nine of the dots with only four straight lines without lifting the pencil off the paper. Many people subconsciously impose another requirement; namely, that the connecting lines must all be within the confines of the nine-dot block. That requirement is not part of the puzzle, and the puzzle cannot be solved that way. Three of the four connecting lines must be drawn partially outside the block. One might say that the solver has to "think outside the block."

This book attempts to accomplish three things: Besides suggesting ways to cope with the enormous financial obligations of the federal government and ways to improve the ratio of producers to eaters, it also outlines a way for ordinary American people to nominate and elect government officials who – because of the way they have been elected – will feel responsible to them alone, instead of to them, to party leaders, and to campaign contributors. None of the solutions proposed is really novel, but most of them do involve a significant departure from the way things are done today.

In the interest of brevity, discussion is limited to the federal government of the United States and the American people, although many of the changes proposed apply about as well to state and local governments and to the governments and peoples of other nations as well. Also, in the interest of simplicity, only masculine pronouns are used throughout.

Table of Contents

INTRODUCTION v

Part I. The Federal Government 1

Chapter 1. Setup for the Fall. 1
  A. Habitual Deficit Spending. 1
  B. Federal Government Debt. 4
  C. Recession and Nascent Recovery. 9
  D. Recovery Inhibitors. 10
  E. Potential Threats to the Nation's Economy. 11

Chapter 2. Alternatives for Managing theFederal
  Budget. 15
  A. Borrow More From the Public. 15
  B. Reduce Social Security and Medicare Benefits. 16
  C. Increase the Payroll Tax Rate or the Earnings
    Base. 21
  D. Increase Income Tax Rates. 22
  E. Monetize the Debt. 24
  F. Improve the Producer to Eater (P/E) Ratio. 25
  G. Reduce Expenses. 25
  H. Combinations of These Seven Alternatives. 29
  I. Default. 30

Chapter 3. A Scenario for Defaulting. 32

Chapter 4. Downsizing, Cost Cutting and Restructur-
  ing. 40
  A. The Size of Government. 40
  B. Reasons for Reducing the Size and Cost of Gov-
    ernment. 42
  C. Guidance. 54

D. Downsize and Cost-Cut the Executive Branch. 59

E. Reorganize and Downsize Congress..................63

F. Downsize the Federal Judicial System..............68

G. Repeal the Federal Income Tax Law and Substitute. 73

Part II. The Producer/Eater Ratio 79

Section A. Optimizing the P/E Pipeline...................79

Chapter 5. Enhancing Environments for Children...84

A. Early Marriages. 84

B. Mothers Stay Home. 87

C. Having It All. 96

D. The Marriage Contract. 100

E. The Marriage License. 103

F. Divorce. 108

G. Better Schooling. 113

Chapter 6. Minimizing Out-of-Wedlock Pregnancies...
119

A. Celibacy. 120

B. Single-sex Educational Institutions. 128

C. Constraints on Women's Dress...................129

D. Contraception.......................................131

E. Abortion. 134

F. Sex Education.......................................135

G. Prostitution. 138

Section B. Reducing the Size of Eater Pools. 144

Chapter 7. Immigrants.......................................144

A. Freeloaders. 144

B. Illegals. 148

Chapter 8. Prisoners......................................153
  A. Prisons...153
  B. Reducing Prison Populations. 157
  C. Alternative Punishments. 160

Chapter 9. Welfare Recipients....................163
  A. Medicare "B." 163
  B. Medicaid...163
  C. Supplemental Security Income.........164
  D. Welfare for Domestic Corporations, Industries
     and Foreign Countries. 164
  E. Welfare for the Poor. 164
  F. Welfare for Incumbent Politicians (Pork). 165

Chapter 10. Life, Death and Killing. 167
  A. Life, What Is It? 167
  B. Death, What Is It? 172

  C. Killing..**179**

Chapter 11. Reducing the Number of Eaters...........182
  A. Abortions...182
  B. Birthed Feticide. 184
  C. Suicide and Assisted Suicide. 187
  D. Euthanasia. 190

Part III. The Electoral System......................193

Chapter 12. The Current Electoral System. 193

**Chapter 13. The Grass Roots Empowerment Electoral
  System.** 197

Part I. The Federal Government

Chapter 1. Setup for the Fall.

A. Habitual Deficit Spending.

A series of prodigal Congresses, bingeing on credit for 43 of the 52 years ending in 2002, has set the stage for a federal government fiscal debacle and brought the nation to the brink of financial ruin. The terrorist destruction of the two World Trade Center buildings on September 11, 2001, caused a late awakening in the nation and forced the federal government into taking action and paying the necessary cost, whatever that may be, to improve homeland security and combat terrorism. Unfortunately, this comes at a time when the federal government has already locked itself into retirement and medical programs that have been increasing in cost and, beginning as early as 2008, will increase in earnest as the baby boomers start to retire. As a consequence, the federal government finds itself in a precarious and deteriorating fiscal situation, vulnerable in a number of ways.

The business cycle, a natural phenomenon of the capitalist system, proceeds roughly as a sine wave. The idea of John Maynard Keynes was that government can smooth out these undulations by borrowing and spending as the economy is retreating, thus compensating for reduced spending by other sectors of the economy. Then, when the economy begins moving upward, the theory goes, government revenue increases, the government reduces spending and, with the surpluses thus created, repays the money it borrowed and positions itself to help out again in the next down cycle. Although this scenario is sound as a theory, it does not work in practice for the federal government because it keeps spending more than the revenue it receives both in good times and in bad.

The federal government's deficit spending did not begin as a regular practice until 1932, and then it continued every year – with few exceptions as noted below– until 1998 when began the first of four years of surplus. **(Figure a.)**

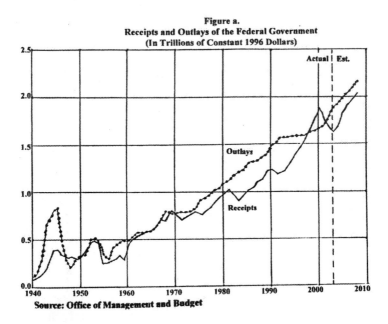

Figure a.
Receipts and Outlays of the Federal Government
(In Trillions of Constant 1996 Dollars)

Source: Office of Management and Budget

The deficits in the 43 years from 1950 through 2002 were caused by increased spending year after year, rather than by reduced revenue. Years with surpluses were 1951, 1956, 1957, 1960, and 1969. Then there was not another surplus year until1998, when there were four in a row: 1998, 1999, 2000, and 2001. Surpluses in those four years resulted from the stock market bubble which produced large capital gains and, in turn, significantly increased federal revenue. Outlays in these four years grew, too, but not as fast. Due to the bursting of the stock market bubble and rising defense and defense-related expenses, deficits began again in the

2

year 2002 and are projected to continue through 2008, the last year that the Office of Management and Budget projects budget data at the time of this writing.

The federal government began its major social programs in 1935 with the Social Security Act as part of President Franklin D. Roosevelt's New Deal Program. In 1965, its social programs were further expanded in a major way by amendments of the Social Security Act to include Medicare, Medicaid and more as part of President Lyndon B. Johnson's Great Society Program. When asked during the Viet Nam War whether the nation could afford guns (defense) or butter (social programs), President Johnson's facile reply was that the nation could afford *both* guns and butter.

There have been costly wars and police actions during the 52 years ending in 2002, but the primary reason for the federal governments impending fiscal crisis is our flawed electoral system. By the time each of the 535 federal legislators gets through introducing new legislation and adding onto appropriation bills to benefit his campaign contributors in hopes of enhancing his own chances of reelection, their combined efforts are almost bound to result in a budget deficit every year. Reelection campaigns are expensive to run, and incumbent legislators get the money to finance them from contributions of those benefitted. The federal government will extricate itself from the impending fiscal crisis by defaulting on some or all of its debts, but the crisis will recur unless our present flawed electoral system is replaced. See Part III.

Consider this: *1.* Nearly constant annual budget deficits for the 52 years ending in 2002; *2.* Large projected annual budget deficits for at least the next five years resulting from increased costs of homeland security and the war on terror; *3.* The increasing number of baby boomers beginning retirement with the concomitant increase in the number of eaters and decrease in the number of producers, which means increased government

3

expenses and very likely decreased revenue. (See Part II for definitions of eaters and producers.); and, finally *4*. The natural propensity of members of Congress to continue deficit spending to improve their own chances of renomination and reelection, The question now is: Can the nation afford rising costs of both guns and butter? It appears that it cannot afford their rising costs now and, in fact, never was able to afford as many guns and as much butter as we have had in the past 52 years.

B. Federal Government Debt.

The federal government is awash in red ink. The natural result of the federal government living beyond its means for years is a large national debt and one that promises to get entirely out of hand in years to come. The federal government has two kinds of debt: debt-*on*-the-books and debt-*off*-the-books. None of the federal government's debts are collateralized; that is, they represent merely the government's promise to pay. For example, if the government fails to pay any of its debts, no creditor is entitled to take over Yellowstone National Park. In addition to these two kinds of debt, potential happenings exist that threaten the fiscal stability of the federal government.

1. Debt On-the-Books.

By the year 2002, the cost of wars and our efforts in the cold war arms race, combined with mounting costs of social programs, the wasteful spending of a profligate Congress on foolish pork barrel projects, subsidies to support inefficient but politically influential industries and some kinds of farming, foreign aid, expensive but mostly fruitless training programs, and similar investments – mostly without return – resulted in $6.2 trillion of booked national debt, which amounted to 60 percent of the gross domestic product (GDP). The Office of Management and Budget (OMB) projects the booked debt to increase to $9.4 trillion by the year 2008, amounting to 68 percent of GDP.

Of the $6.2 trillion of debt on the books in the year 2002, federal accounts such as the Social Security and Medicare trust funds held $2.7 trillion, and the Federal Reserve System held $604 billion. The U.S. Treasury has sold securities worldwide on the open market in the amount of $2.9 trillion to individuals, banks, insurance companies, and other institutions. Banks, insurance companies, and other such institutions with huge amounts of money to invest have actually benefitted from securities sold by the Treasury because the Treasury securities give them a place to invest these large sums with very little risk and a reasonable return. Nobody is much concerned about this $2.9 trillion of publicly-held debt because the Treasury manages it quite easily. When there is not enough money in the general fund to pay off maturing securities, the Treasury has been able to roll the debt over by selling additional securities with later maturities on the open market, or to borrow from the trust funds. It can use part of the proceeds from these sales to pay off the securities that have come due, and the government can spend the rest. Or the Treasury can sell securities to the Federal Reserve Board. The FRB creates the money to pay for them, thus increasing the money supply, cheapening the dollar, contributing to future inflation, and partially monetizing the debt (as in Alternative e, Chapter 2).

2. Debt Off-the-Books.

Besides the $2.9 trillion of publicly-held debt on-the-books of the Treasury in the year 2002, the federal government had debt off-the-books in the form of enormous obligations under various programs to pay benefits to retirees. Principal among these are Old Age and Survivors Insurance (OASI), Disability Insurance

(DI), and Hospital "A" Insurance (HI). (OASI and DI were on-the-books until 1985, when the Balanced Budget and Emergency Deficit Control Act of 1985 [Public Law 99-177] decreed that they be off-the-books.) Other smaller programs are military and civilian government employee retirement annuities, and the railroad employee retirement annuity. In each of these cases, the government receives monthly payments from participants during the period of their employment. In return, the government has promised to pay benefits to them during the period of their retirement or disability, and to their survivors in accordance with the provisions of the Social Security Act of 1935, as amended.

Payments to OASI, DI and Medicare "A" (HI) beneficiaries are currently made out of receipts from payroll taxes, from income taxes levied on Social Security benefits, and from interest the Treasury pays to these trust funds on funds borrowed from them. When receipts from these sources exceed payments to Social Security and Medicare "A" beneficiaries, the Treasury borrows the excess from the OASI, DI, and HI trust funds, adds it to the general fund, and the government spends it to pay for the government's share of Supplementary Medical Insurance (SMI) costs (and, at times, for purposes unrelated to Social Security and Medicare).

When the Treasury borrows from the trust funds, it issues securities to the funds in return. By the year 2002, Social Security OASDI (Old Age and Survivors and Disability Insurance) and Medicare trust funds held such securities in an amount totaling $1.6 trillion. (Treasury securities held by all federal government accounts such as Social Security and Medicare trust funds all together totaled $2.7 trillion). These securities are backed by the full faith and credit of the federal government, but unlike the securities the Treasury sells to the public, those issued to the trust funds cannot be sold. They are merely accounting IOU's issued for bookkeeping purposes and are only redeemable by the Treasury.

The cost of SMI is funded about 75 percent from the Treasury's general fund and about 25 percent from monthly premiums paid by beneficiaries. At this time, the 75 percent paid by the Treasury is offset by surpluses in OASI, DI, and HI, so that the income and benefit payments for all of OASDI, HI and SMI, taken together, are roughly in balance. But the OASDI and HI surpluses will diminish in the future when escalating payments to Social Security and Medicare beneficiaries exceed income. This is certain to happen. During the 20 years preceding the year 2000, the number of Old Age and Survivors and Disability Insurance OASDI beneficiaries increased by 10 million. During the 20 years after the year 2000, the number is expected to increase by 23 million as the baby boom generation retires. **(Figure b)**. Medicare costs will also continue to grow rapidly due to the expected increasing use and cost of health care. Then the Treasury will have to make payments in the amount of the shortfalls out of the general fund, adding greatly to pressure on the federal budget. The shortfalls would be exacerbated if there were an increase in unemployment, causing a reduction in receipts from the payroll tax. The Medicare prescription drug benefit program – recently enacted into law – will certainly increase pressure on the Treasury.

The National Center for Policy Analysis (NCPA) headquartered in Dallas, Texas, calculates that, as of the year 2001, the accumulated entitlement obligations owed to all people (including all current workers) who have earned Social Security and Medicare benefits is $12.9 trillion and $16.9 trillion, respectively. Combined with debt held by the public, the debt comes to about $33 trillion. These numbers appear to include Medicare "B" but do not include unfunded federal employee retirement and other similar but lesser obligations. A study commissioned by former Secretary of the Treasury, Paul O'Neal and completed in 2003 determined the net future budget deficit to be at least $44 trillion. These implicit commitments of $37 trillion for Medicare and $7

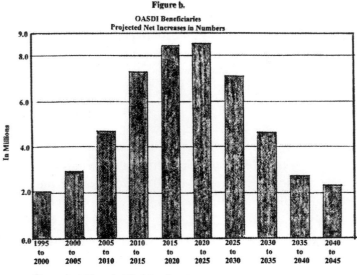

Figure b.

OASDI Beneficiaries
Projected Net Increases in Numbers

Source: Social Security Administration

trillion for Social Security dwarf the debt carried on the Treasury's books. On May 29, 2003, the *Financial Times,* London Edition, reported that the Bush administration suppressed the report, but the administration denies this.The fiscal year 2004 budget of the U. S. Government includes the Social Security Administration's reported calculations of a net long-term deficit of $18 trillion for Social Security and Medicare. Combined with debt held by the public, the total comes to about $21 trillion. All three of these amounts are calculated in different ways, and are based on somewhat different assumptions. For example, the Social Security Administration's calculations are based on the assumption that the Treasury has the funds to pay the trust funds for the securities they hold. Although the Social Security Administration must assume this in making its calculations, the Treasury does not actually have the funds. All three of these calculations are only as accurate as the assumptions that go into them. Really accurate obligations cannot be known until terms are laid down and actuarial calculations are made, similar to those described in Chapter 3.

The federal government includes in the $6.2 trillion it carried on its books as national debt in 2002 only the $2.7 trillion that it had borrowed from federal accounts – principally the Social Security and Medicare trust funds. None of these three figures ($33 trillion, $44 trillion, or $21 trillion) is carried on the Treasury's books as debt. However, these huge figures are not in themselves a cause for alarm because, like federally issued bonds and notes, these are debts that will become due and payable over a period of years. In the case of Social Security and Medicare liabilities, they are usually calculated for a period of 75 years. Bonds are for 30 years. What is important is that these huge off-the-books debts must be serviced the same as bonds, notes, and bills that are carried on the Treasury's books.

To put the federal government's combined on-the-books and off-the-books debt in perspective, it is between two and four times the size of the nation's gross domestic product and between 10 and 20 times the size of the federal government's gross annual income, depending upon which of these three debt calculations one accepts.

C. Recession and Nascent Recovery.

At the time of this writing, the economy is just recovering from the recession following the bursting of the stock market bubble and the September 11, 2001 terrorist destruction of the World Trade Center buildings, but it appears to be recovering nicely. The executive and legislative branches have taken vigorous action to revive the economy by reducing federal income taxes, and the Federal Reserve Board has cooperated by lowering the federal funds rate to an historic low level and liberally increasing the money supply. Lower taxes result in consumers having more money to spend, and spending it boosts the economy. The result of the low federal funds rate is low short term interest rates, which encourages consumers to buy cars, appliances, and the like. The results of the liberal money supply have been to lower long-term interest rates, including mortgage rates, which encourages consumers to buy houses. Businesses are likewise encouraged to invest in capital equipment.

If these efforts are successful and the economy responds as hoped, the day of reckoning for the federal government could be postponed for some time. If the economy does not respond as hoped, it could lapse back into recession. An economy in recession would mean reduced federal government revenue which would, in turn, accelerate the day when the government cannot meet its financial obligations.

D. Recovery Inhibitors.

There are two factors or conditions that are probably impeding or frustrating the federal government's efforts to revive the economy:

1. It is not only the federal government that is deeply in debt. Many state and local governments are deeply in debt as well. California is, of course, the prime example, and New York State is a close second. State and local governments are doing all they can to improve their financial situations by increasing state and local taxes and fees wherever possible, and these efforts are detracting to some degree from efforts made by the federal government to revive the economy. Consumer credit in 2003 has never been so high. It stands now at close to $2 trillion. Low interest rates prompted many home buyers to refinance the mortgages on their homes, take out money, and thereby reduce their home equity. Much if not most of this money was spent.

Early in the year 2003, household debt (including mortgages) amounted to about $8.7 trillion or 108 percent of income. Credit card debt is about $735 billion. Personal and business bankruptcies are increasing. Personal bankruptcies currently stand at about 1.5 million a year. The significance of all this is that businesses and consumers deeply in debt are likely to curtail the consumer purchasing that has been sustaining the economy in recent years.

2. So far, the recovery has been without significant gains in employment. The exportation of jobs must surely be an impediment to reducing unemployment. At first, it was low-skilled jobs in manufacturing that were exported. More recently, industries importuned government to issue visas for skilled employees to take jobs in the United States. Unions often complained that people with the necessary skills were already here in this country, but the rub was that they demanded higher wages than workers coming to the U.S. on work visas. Of late, the service industry has discovered that highly technical jobs and clerical jobs can be handled over the Internet by technicians and clerks in foreign countries like India, Ireland, and China without having to seek visas for foreign employees. Reportedly, 2.5 million manufacturing jobs have been exported during the past couple of years. Most of the jobs that have been lost will never return, and the resulting effect on the economy is to pull it down because, as a rule, the unemployed have diminished purchasing power.

E. Potential Threats to the Nation's Economy.

The existing proclivity of Congress for deficit spending plus financing the cost of combating terrorism and baby boomer retirements will be enough to eventually put the federal government down financially, but any of the following six potential happenings

11

would adversely affect the economy and hasten the time that a federal budget crunch occurs:

1. Of the approximate $3 trillion of publicly-held federal debt in the year 2003, approximately $1.3 trillion or about 42 percent was foreign-owned. Japan owned $440 billion, China $122 billion, and the remainder was owned by more than a dozen other countries. The sheer size of foreign-held debt creates a certain vulnerability for the U.S. government. China and Japan would be reluctant to sell the Treasury securities they now hold for fear of depressing the U.S. economy, their major market. But should they do so or should foreign countries even refrain from buying Treasury securities in the quantities that they have been (about $1.5 billion per day), there would be serious consequences for the federal government which now receives a significant portion of its income from these sales. But this could happen if the dollar were significantly devalued. Interest rates on new securities sold by the Treasury would increase, causing the value of securities now held by foreign central banks and institutions to decline. Should there thus be large sales of foreign-held Treasury securities, the dollar proceeds from the sales would be converted to the currency of the foreign country, contributing further to a cheaper dollar and to inflation in the United States.

2. The federal government provides insurance and guarantees in a number of forms. The Federal Deposit Insurance Corporation is an example. Banks pay premiums to the federal government to insure the accounts of depositors up to a certain amount against bank failure. The government may become liable for huge expenses in the event of extensive bank meltdowns. In a situation similar to what could happen to banks, the Federal Savings and Loan Deposit Insurance became liable for well over a hundred billion dollars in the 1980's when the savings and loan institutions suffered liquidity problems. The Pension Benefit Guarantee Corporation is another similar example. There are others. Any one of these insurance or guarantee programs, if called upon, might not be able to meet heavy demands on them with their relatively meager resources and may require bailout by the Treasury.

3. James B. Stack, writing in the July 2003, issue of *Inves-Tech Research,* speculates that a rapid rise in interest rates or a collapse of the dollar could create a situation in which traders in the United States would find it impossible to unwind huge positions in the derivatives (options, futures, and the like) market, causing it to meltdown. Just such a financial crisis did occur in 1998, when the Long Term Capital Management hedge fund misjudged the market. The fund would have gone belly-up with drastic repercussions for the U.S. economy were it not for the Federal Reserve's call to the international banking establishment to refloat the fund, which it did. Many banks and insurance companies deal in derivatives as a source of income – albeit a risky one – to compensate for low interest income. Warren Buffett, "the Sage of Omaha" and CEO of Berkshire Hathaway, Inc. in his letter transmitting the company's 2002 annual report, referred to derivatives as "financial weapons of mass destruction, carrying dangers that, while now latent, are potentially lethal."

4. Many people believe that there is a currently-existing real estate bubble. If, indeed, we are now experiencing such a bubble and it bursts like the stock market bubble did in 2001, the result would be the recessing of the economy, similar to that which followed the stock market bubble. Some home buyers who found themselves in possession of a property of a lesser value than the amount they still owed on it would walk away leaving the bank with the property and a nonperforming loan. If there were much of this, banks would find themselves in difficulty. Local governments

heavily dependent on real estate taxes for revenue would also find themselves in hot water.

5. Another major terrorist attack like the destruction of the World Trade Center on September 11, 2001 would likely cause the stock market to react in a way similar to what it did then and, probably, the economy along with it.

6. The Organization of Petroleum Exporting Countries (OPEC) cartel controls the supply of oil in the world with a fair degree of effectiveness. The United States now imports about 60 percent of the oil that it consumes. Should OPEC decide to – and be able to – restrict the world's supply of oil, the American economy would be adversely affected because of the nation's high degree of dependency on imported oil. The OPEC oil embargo of 1973 did just that, and at that time the United States was only dependent on imports of foreign oil for only about 30 percent of the oil it consumes.

Any of these potential happenings – and there may be others – could cause the federal government to be unable to pay its bills much earlier than that time would otherwise occur.

Chapter 2. Alternatives for Managing the Federal Budget.

Besides efforts to revive the economy, the federal government has at its disposal the alternatives listed below which can be used to manage the budget and stave off the fateful day.

A. Borrow More From the Public.

Of the various alternatives open to the federal government, this is likely to be the principal one selected, because it is the path of least resistance. As costs continue to grow and when there is not enough money in the general fund to pay the bills as they come due, the Treasury will sell securities to the public on the open market to the extent that it needs to and to the extent that it is able to, in order to accommodate the additional costs. However, as the debt increases, lenders will demand higher interest rates to compensate them for the higher risk they take in lending increasing amounts to the government, causing further increases in the cost of the debt.

The Federal Reserve Board, highly effective in controlling short-term interest rates, is much less effective in controlling long-term interest rates which are determined largely by the marketplace. As the government increases its borrowing from the public, funds that could have been invested in plant and infrastructure will be drawn off, making borrowing more expensive for business and tending to depress the economy and, thence, government revenue. Long-term interest rates have already begun to increase at the time of this writing.

B. Reduce Social Security and Medicare Benefits.

If the government is legally able to do so, it may continue to reduce benefits a little at a time. The government has reduced benefits a little at a time before on a number of occasions without legal challenge and without unduly upsetting beneficiaries. The government could also increase the age of full retirement. The age of full retirement was increased recently from 65 to 67 over a period of years. The government could reduce or delay cost-of -living adjustments, or lay additional income taxes on Social Security income, which was originally tax free. Beneficiaries could be means tested to reduce the number qualifying for benefits. As the government sees it, benefits could be drastically reduced legally in any or all of these ways. Legal or not, reducing benefits is a step that legislators recognize as being politically risky.

Many people have come to view Social Security as a Ponzi scheme. Charles A. Ponzi was a swindler who operated a pyramid (also known as pay-as-you-go, or chain letter) type scheme that defrauded thousands of people of millions of dollars after World War I. He promised huge returns to people who gave him their money to invest. He did not invest the money, but used the money of later contributors instead to maintain a lavish lifestyle and to pay off earlier contributors with handsome profits. People clamored to give him their money. Like all such schemes, money coming in eventually did not keep up with his obligations to earlier contributors. He went broke and went to prison in 1920 for his fraudulent and illegal scheme. Like Ponzi's scheme, Social Security is pay-as-you-go and bears some of the earmarks of the Ponzi scheme, such as using income for purposes unrelated to Social Security and Medicare, and a transparent effort to conceal the biggest part of the government's debt by carrying it off the books. Officials at the Enron Corporation may have taken lessons from the federal government when it came to recording debt off the company's books.

Other people view OASI, DI, and HI insurance as annuities; that is, they think of them as contracts between individual workers and the federal government in which the worker (along with his employer) employed in most occupations has been forced by law to pay – and in good faith has paid – premiums (consideration) dictated by the government. In return, the federal government promised to and should be similarly bound legally to pay the worker for retirement, disability, and hospital benefits after he reaches the age of 65 (in some cases, earlier and, in some cases, later) in accordance with the terms of the contract.

Of these two views, the federal government subscribes to the former. Well, not exactly. It regards Social Security as a *legalized* Ponzi Scheme. Relying on a U.S. Supreme Court case *Flemmimg v. Nestor*, 1960. (363 US 603, 4 L Ed 2d, 80 Sct 1367), the federal government's position is that OASI, DI, and HI insurances are not annuity contracts, and beneficiaries have no property rights in these programs. The government concludes that these are *nudum pactums* or naked agreements without consideration and, hence, legally unenforceable by retirees receiving benefits. Thus, as the federal government views the Social Security and Medicare "A" programs, it is legally able to cancel the programs altogether if it chooses to do so. It owes nothing and need pay nothing to covered retirees.

Accordingly, the Chairman of the Federal Reserve Board, a few federal legislators, and some journalists have advocated reducing substantially – or perhaps radically – Social Security and Medicare benefits as a way of resolving the federal government's upcoming fiscal crisis. This would place the entire burden of resolving the upcoming crisis exclusively on the backs of the nation's current and soon-to-be retirees receiving Social Security and Medicare benefits, although these are the people least able

17

to bear it. Other journalists have advocated means testing for Social Security and Medicare recipients as a way for determining which recipients should be paid and which should not. However, nobody has been heard to advocate that banks and other holders of Treasury securities should not be paid in full or that they should be means tested to determine which of them should be paid and which should not.

In the *Flemming* case, Nestor was an alien who was deported as a member of the Communist Party at a time when being a member of the Communist party was a crime, and OASI benefits were denied him as a deportee in accordance with Section 202(n) of the Social Security Act. Nestor prevailed in the lower court, but the government appealed to the U.S. Supreme Court. That Supreme Court held that Nestor's right to OASI benefits could not properly be considered to be of the order of an accrued property right because the eligibility for benefits, and the amount of such benefits, do not in any true sense depend on contributions to the program through the payment of taxes, but rather on the earnings record of the primary beneficiary. For this reason, the court concluded that the non-contractual interest of an employee covered by the Act cannot be soundly analogized to that of a holder of an annuity, whose right to benefits is bottomed on his contractual premium payments. A direct relationship does exist between the amount of payroll taxes paid by the primary beneficiary and the amount of benefits to which he is entitled, but the court concluded that these payments do not equate to annuity insurance premiums. One might say that the court based its opinion on a technicality.

The court noted in its decision that Congress may not exercise its power to modify the statutory scheme of the Social Security Act free of all constitutional restraint. The court observed that the interest of a covered employee under the Act is of sufficient substance to fall within the protection from arbitrary governmental action afforded by the due process clause of the U.S. Constitution.

The court also noted that the original Social Security Act contained a clause, still in force, that expressly reserves to Congress the right to alter, amend, or repeal any provisions of the Act.

In a strongly-worded dissent, Justice Black contended that the Court's holding equated OASI, DI, and Medicare "A" benefit recipients to those individuals covered by programs such as Medicaid who receive benefits but pay nothing. He also suggested that the decision did not follow *Lynch v. United States* where the U.S. Supreme Court unanimously held that Congress was without power to repudiate and abrogate in whole or in part its promises to pay amounts claimed by soldiers under the War Risk Insurance Act of 1917 because such a repudiation would be inconsistent with the due process clause of the U.S. Constitution. Justice Black, noting that Congress properly retained the right to alter, amend, or repeal any provisions of the Act, maintained that this reservation applied only with respect to the future; that is, that the government could stop covering new people or even stop increasing its obligations to those already covered, but that is quite another thing from stopping or reducing benefits to those already covered which would amount to a taking proscribed by the due process clause.

Here's what President Franklin Delano Roosevelt, who was responsible for enactment of the Social Security Act, said about Social Security payroll contributions:

> *We put those payroll contributions there so as to give the contributors a legal, moral, and political right to collect their pensions and unemployment benefits.*

If the government did significantly reduce Social Security or Medicare "A" benefits and a noncommunist, resident citizen qualified for such benefits, brought a lawsuit claiming breach of contract, it is possible that the U.S. Supreme Court, as constituted today, might reverse Flemming v. Nestor. But, whether or not a beneficiary does bring a suit challenging the federal government's right to reduce OASI, DI, and HI benefits – and regardless of how the courts might rule on such a case if brought – the federal government must regard OASI, DI, and HI as annuity contracts and beneficiaries as annuitants. Here's why: Social Security plays a critical role in the lives of 46 million beneficiaries, and over 150 million covered workers and their families. These millions of people will regard a substantial reduction in their Social Security or Medicare "A" benefits as a default by the federal government in the payment of its debts, even if the U.S. Supreme Court does not. They will do this the same as bankers would if their Treasury bonds were not paid on time and in full. There would be a national uproar, and many elected officials then in office would suffer the consequences during the first national election thereafter. Lawmakers know this and seek to delay the day of reckoning so that it occurs on somebody else's watch after they have left office. That is why Social Security has been termed the third rail of politics, and that is why no serious effort has been made so far to come to grips with this problem.

There is only one way that such a national uproar might possibly be avoided and that is if OASI, DI, and HI beneficiaries correctly perceive (1) that they are getting a fair shake at the time; that is, that their share is the best that the federal government is able to provide under existing circumstances; (2) that they are being treated the same as others with whom the federal government owes contractual obligations (such as holders of Treasury securities, federal government and railroad employee retirees); *and* (3) that they are being treated better than others who the federal government pays but to whom it has no contractual obligation.

Why is it important whether or not OASI, DI, and Medicare "A" are considered to be annuity contracts? The first obligation of the federal government is to defend the country, including the war against terrorism and homeland security. The second obligation of the federal government is to veterans particularly to combat veterans who have risked their lives and limbs to make it possible for the federal government to fulfill its primary responsibility of defending the nation. Beyond that, its other obligations can be arbitrarily classified into third and fourth categories. The third category, in order of priority, is contractual obligations and binding treaty obligations of the federal government, and fourth, "all other" costs and obligations. The "all other" category would include the cost of running the three branches of government, Supplemental Security Income (SSI), Medicaid and all other subsidies, grants and welfare programs.

Because the federal government's obligations for Social Security and Medicare are so huge, it will not be possible to pay them as they come due at some point in the future. Consequently, OASI, DI, and Medicare "A" beneficiaries are bound to suffer painful reductions in benefits that they have come to expect and to which most beneficiaries believe they are entitled. This is certain, but if OASI, DI, and HI are categorized as annuity contracts – instead of being categorized as "all other" obligations – they should be treated the same as Treasury bonds, notes, and bills held by the public. Losses sustained by those in the third category should be proportionately much less than the losses of those in the fourth category. Every expense in the fourth category should be either cut to the bone or eliminated entirely.

C. Increase the Payroll Tax Rate or the Earnings Base.

The payroll tax rate has been increased a number of times in the past with the largest increase (from 9.35 percent to 14 percent, including taxes paid by the employer) taking effect in 1984. The current payroll tax for Social Security – including amounts paid by the employee and by the employer for the employee – is 12.4 percent. Add to that the payroll tax of 2.9 percent for Medicare "A", and the total is 15.3 percent. The payroll tax is now about as high as is practical. Nearly three-quarters of American workers pay more in payroll taxes than they do in income taxes. The earnings base for OASI and DI has usually been adjusted annually to reflect increases in average wages and is now up to about $87,000. There is no base upper limit for Medicare "A".

D. Increase Income Tax Rates.

Federal taxes already amount to 17.9 percent of the GDP, and income tax rates, rather than being increased, have recently been decreased in an effort to stimulate the economy. Some studies have shown that increasing tax rates much more would generally be fruitless, because the economy begins to diminish so that with the higher tax rate applied to a lower base, the amount of taxes collected would remain about the same. In 1940, the total receipts of the federal government totaled $6.5 billion with about one-third of that coming from excise taxes. Revenue grew. By 2002, federal government receipts from various sources totaled $1.8 trillion. Of this total, about 50 percent came from the personal income tax and 35 percent from the payroll tax. Referendums in a couple of states recently on increasing state taxes have failed by large majorities, indicating that voters are not favorably inclined to tax increases.

Tax rates are already high. Consider the amount of every person's paycheck that is deducted for federal, state, and local income taxes. Consider also the amount deducted from his paycheck in the way of payroll tax for Social Security and Medicare *and* the corresponding amount the employer pays which otherwise would appropriately be paid to the employee. Out of the amount that remains, the individual must pay real and personal property taxes, sales taxes, cigarette taxes, gasoline taxes, utility taxes, state and local automobile license fees, and more. The total tax burden is calculated in different ways by different analytical organizations which come up with somewhat different results, but most of the calculations hover around one-third of the average worker's income.

We pay out still more of the amount that remains when government passes laws and issues regulations not considered to be taxes but which result in increased prices for us. These price increases are the same as tax increases; that is, the money is taken from us the same as if it were labeled a tax. For example, before the increase in the minimum wage that preceded the last one, two orders of hot cakes and sausage and two senior citizen coffees cost $3.95 at the local McDonald's restaurant. After this increase, the price jumped to $4.37, an increase of $0.42. Another example is the universal service charge added to our telephone bills to pay for rural telephone services and providing computer capabilities in schools. The additional costs don't sound like a lot but, together, they add up.

We also pay through unnecessarily increased costs of government. This is a frequent occurrence when elected politicians require the executive branch to create unneeded government jobs for unqualified and poorly qualified campaign workers as a reward for the services (often unpaid or underpaid) of those workers rendered during the politicians' campaigns for election. When this happens, government services are degraded because the campaign workers are not required to have civil service system qualifications and are often not qualified for the jobs they get. When the administration changes, many of these people remain by acquiring civil service status through one means or another (burrowing into the woodwork, it is called). Anytime the government hires an employee who does not meet civil service requirements and is not the best qualified of those candidates available, government efficiency is decreased from what it would have been, and costs are unnecessarily increased. It is the taxpayer who pays.

E. Monetize the Debt.

When it is not possible or practical to sell more securities to federal accounts or to the public, the federal government can resort to monetizing some of its debts by borrowing from the Federal Reserve System. The Federal Reserve literally creates the money to pay for the securities it buys, thus increasing the money supply which, in turn, leads to inflation. Moderate inflation has been very useful to the federal government and to all debtors in the United States for paying off debts in dollars cheaper than they were at the time the debts were incurred. However, this can be carried to an extreme as it was in Germany during the early twenties where it dragged on for years. It is said that near the end it took an armload of mark notes to buy a loaf of bread. In lieu of a viable medium of exchange, people resorted to barter. The mark eventually became worthless and had to be replaced. Although monetizing may have worked for a time in Germany, it may not be of much help at this time in the United States because Social Security obligations have inflation indexing built in so that Social Security costs will rise with inflation. Medicare costs are rising faster than the Consumer Price Index (CPI) now and are expected to continue to do so in the future. Fortunately, the federal debt owed to the public is denominated in U.S. dollars so, theoretically at least, the government could pay off securities held by the public (including foreign creditors) through galloping inflation if it wished to do so, but there would be serious unwanted side effects.

F. Improve the Producer to Eater (P/E) Ratio.

Create an environment conducive to reducing the number of eaters in the economy and to improving the chances of children in the pipeline becoming adult producers. Steps required to create such an environment are described in Part II.

G. Reduce Expenses.

Government expenses should be reduced. The president and Congress have unsuccessfully aspired more than once to balance the budget by legislating ceilings on the national debt carried on the Treasury's books, but the debt ceiling has served as no impediment at all. Congress simply raises it from time to time as needed to accommodate additional annual budget deficits.

Assuming that the Congress was able to reduce expenses significantly, where exactly should expenses be reduced? The federal government divides its expenditures into five categories: National Defense, Human Resources, Net Interest, Physical Resources, and Other. Only the first three categories are shown on **Figure c** because the amounts spent for the last two are considerably smaller than the amounts spent for the first three. Notice from **Figure c** that the distribution of federal government expenditures has changed over the years. Expenditures for human resources have increased steadily since 1932. Now, nearly 60 percent of total federal government expenditures go for the human resources function which includes education, training, employment services, social services, health, income security, Social Security, and veteran's benefits and services. This is four times the amount spent for national defense and nearly eight times the amount paid out for interest. What is alarming about the rapidly rising human resources expenses is the knowledge that in years to come these

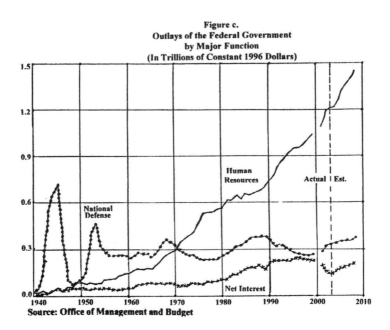

Figure c.
Outlays of the Federal Government
by Major Function
(In Trillions of Constant 1996 Dollars)

Source: Office of Management and Budget

expenses will rise at a much faster rate as the baby boomers begin to retire.

Since human resource programs are the most costly, could cuts be made there? For example, could veterans benefits be cut? If we want armed forces in the future that will be there to defend the country, it would not be wise to slack off much on veterans' benefits, and particularly on benefits for wounded veterans and veterans who have served in actual combat. Could Medicaid be terminated or drastically curtailed? If so, what will happen to old people in nursing homes? Would they be put out on the street? Surely the Congress would not consider cutting Medicaid programs that benefit children?

How would aged people on Social Security and Medicare live if these programs were drastically cut back? Retired federal government civilian and military employees might not be able to sustain themselves if their retirement benefits were drastically curtailed. Single mothers with dependent children could not survive once the many social programs designed to support her and her children were drastically cut back. In summary, the consequences of significant reductions in this category of expenditure would seem to be dire indeed.

Defense of the nation is the primary mission of the federal government, and today the security of the nation and its people are being threatened by terrorists. It doesn't seem logical to cut back on that function. To the contrary, funds appropriated for national defense may have to be increased in coming years. Cutting interest payments would certainly amount to default.

Could cuts be made in the "other functions" category? For example, would dairy farmers be able to survive without a subsidy? How about the peanut farmer? The sugar cane farmer? The steel industry? The truth is that over the years, large segments of American families, industries and agriculture have become dependent on the federal government dole, and the consequences of its withdrawal or drastic curtailment in almost any area are not pleasant to contemplate.

Why are so many dependent on the federal dole? There are at least two reasons. The first reason is that, in return for campaign contributions and votes, the government has enacted various kinds of legislation to subsidize inefficient businesses, industries, individuals and groups. This is pork barrel (shortened to just "pork") legislation. Once subsidized, these entities need no longer strive to become competitive because their existence is assured by governmental largesse. They remain inefficient and continue to depend on the largesse.

The second reason is that the government has enacted many varied and expensive programs in forming a social safety net, a concept that has been in vogue for some years. In fairness to incumbent legislators, most of them surely see themselves having as their primary motivation in enacting such compassion legislation the rescuing of unfortunate people from the rigors of poverty. At the same time, legislators cannot be unaware that, in the process of forming the safety net, the legislation they enact is pork because it builds for themselves voting constituencies of a huge mass of voters, but voters who are dependent on the federal government. Having so many dependent upon the federal government creates a dangerous economic situation because the federal government is itself the biggest debtor of all and a slender reed upon which to lean in time of need.

The government's monetary policy is likely to be the cause of there being more candidates for the dole in the future. People who have savings can rely on their own resources in time of need. Those who don't have savings --and those, in particular, who are in debt – must rely on the government in time of need. The savings rate for people in this country is lower than it is in any other industrialized country. The main reason is because the federal government has been discouraging saving and encouraging indebtedness. It has been doing it in two ways. First, the Federal Reserve Board has increased the money supply excessively year after year causing ever-present inflation to one degree or another. Inflation penalizes savers by systematically reducing the purchasing power of their savings, but it rewards debtors by enabling them to pay off their debts in cheap, inflated dollars. Those who go into debt to buy investments such as real property and stocks are usually further rewarded by inflation as those investments increase in price. People see this, of course, and some would-be savers join the ranks of the indebted to avoid the penalties and reap the rewards.

Second, during the last few years, the FRB has reduced short term interest rates to historically low levels which have created an incentive for people to go into debt. For example, some individuals with decent credit ratings have been able to take out 60-month loans with a zero percent interest rate to buy new cars, a deal hard to refuse. Reflecting low short term rates, mortgage interest rates have also been low which has served as encouragement for those who already have mortgages on their homes to refinance and take out equity, thereby increasing debt. According to a study done by economists at the Federal Reserve Bank of New York, $5 trillion of home mortgages were refinanced during the period 2001-2003, and equity of $450 billion was taken out. About a quarter of this amount was used to repay or consolidate other debt, but the rest was spent for vacations, autos, home improvements, second homes and the like. These low rates have also been an incentive for families to begin buying their first homes and assuming new debt in lieu of continuing to rent.

H. Combinations of These Seven Alternatives.

The near future appears to be one of rolling over parts of the existing debt as necessary and possible, continuing to increase the debt by borrowing more as necessary and possible, making minor reductions in Social Security and Medicare benefits, increasing the money supply as necessary and possible, and continuing to saddle American producer-taxpayers with high costs for servicing debt ($777 billion). In 2002, the federal government paid $171 billion of interest to service securities issued by the Treasury, $454 billion in Social Security payments and $152 billion for Medicare hospitalization payments. On top of the cost of servicing the debts of the federal government, American producer-taxpayers will continue to be saddled with the costs of financing the federal government's many and varied social and subsidy programs. Can this go on indefinitely? Not likely.

Looked at another way, without the cost of servicing debt (and with other things remaining the same), year 2002 federal taxes could have been reduced by 39 percent ($777 billion/ $2,011 billion in federal outlays = 39%). Taking into account

29

the cost of financing the federal government's many social and subsidy programs, federal taxes could have been cut even more – probably, by well over fifty percent. Such a tax reduction would have been most welcome to young, producer-taxpaying couples struggling to rear children.

I. Default.

Default is better characterized as a last resort rather than an alternative because it will be selected as a course of action only when all else has failed. A corporation in extremis and unable to pay its bills would grasp the nettle, enter Chapter 11 bankruptcy, have all or some of its debts expunged, and reemerge as perhaps a smaller but stronger company. There is, of course, no Chapter 11 bankruptcy provision for governments, but a default is about the equivalent. In the end, this is what the federal government will do. Although it is humiliating to think of the government of the United States of America having to default on its debts like a third-world banana republic, some form of at least a partial default is inevitable sooner or later. For years we have enjoyed the benefits of the federal government overextending itself, but the time is coming to pay the piper.

Defaulting on a part of the debt will be a fiscal calamity not only for this country but for many other countries as well, because they use the dollar as a store of value. However, it will not be the end for the United States. It will be a new beginning. The adjustment will be over and done with all at once. The nation will still have its highly productive work force and its powerful armed forces. Everyone will know where they stand and what losses they will have to take. They will be able to plan and get on with their businesses and their lives. Like many corporations emerging from a Chapter 11 bankruptcy, the nation will be financially stronger than when it entered the process and will be fully capable of coping with its remaining debts. Of course, there will be significant unwanted side effects that cannot be avoided.

Chapter 3. A Scenario for Defaulting.

As the years pass and the cost of government and the debt continue to increase, the problem will get worse, and dealing with it at some indeterminate time in the future will be more difficult than dealing with it now. The best time to implement the proposed scenario would be to get it over with immediately, but for political reasons, that is not possible. The next best time – and the only possible time – is when the federal government is unable to pay its bills as they come due and there is no other way. The time when the federal government cannot pay its bills may be delayed for some time but cannot be avoided. Its debts are simply too big.

This scenario would be executed in six steps. The actuarial calculations needed for the first five steps should begin early enough to be ready when a decision is made to implement the sixth step. The sixth step should begin later as indicated above. For purposes of the scenario, costs would be divided into the four principal categories described earlier. Category one (defense and related costs) and category two (veterans' benefits) should be fully funded. Category three (contractual and binding treaty obligations) would be those costs associated with servicing and paying off the nation's total contractual debt. The debt would be paid off in 360 monthly installments (much like payments are made monthly to pay off a mortgage-secured promissory note on a person's house) with most of it going for interest in the early years and very little for payment of principal. As the years passed and the debt was being paid off, more of the annual payments would go for principal and less for interest. The amount available for the fourth category ("all other" costs) would be calculated by subtracting the costs of the first three categories from the federal government's estimated revenue (receipts) each year. These would be the amounts that Congress could appropriate each year for each category.

The first step, to begin immediately, would be to develop the computer programs necessary to calculate the federal government's liability to each and every creditor using the criteria proposed in step 2, test the programs for accuracy and produce a preliminary estimate of liability as of a given date.

The second step of the scenario would be to calculate the federal government's contractual obligations. Obligations to OASI and DI retirees on Social Security would be calculated on the basis of their life expectancy and the annual annuity payments they are currently receiving, plus an increase for inflation-indexing in the amount of the average annual increase in the Consumer Price Index over the last ten years. Obligations to those who have paid into Social Security but who are not yet drawing benefits would be the amount that they and their employers have paid into Social Security, plus four percent interest a year over the period payments were made. The calculations for active and retired railroad, federal military and civilian employees would be calculated in the same way as for Social Security but with an additional factor for benefits.

Obligations for Medicare "A" recipients would be calculated on the basis of the average payout to Medicare "A" recipients per year and the individual's life expectancy. Obligations for those paying into Medicare "A" but who are not yet eligible for benefits would be calculated in the same way as for Social Security. When these calculations have been completed, the exact amount of the federal government's obligations for OASI, DI, Medicare A, railroad retirement and federal employee retirement debt would be known.

Obligations for all of the securities previously issued to the public by the Treasury and extant at the time would be at their face value. Securities held by the trust funds would be cancelled, and those held by the Federal Reserve Board (FRB) would be left undisturbed.

The third step would be to express all of the federal government's contractual obligations in a common denominator. A common denominator for payments would have to be agreed upon in actual practice, but for this scenario the common denominator for all debt (except that owed to the FRB) would be new 30-year, callable, tradeable, and inheritable Treasury bonds, bearing an interest rate of four percent. All of these new bonds would be identical and would be callable based on a monthly lottery (except for those held by the FRB). The target would be to call enough of the bonds monthly so that all of them would be paid off in 30 years. If an owner felt he could not wait for his bonds to come up on the lottery for payoff, he could sell all or part of them in the open market for cash. Retired and disabled individuals receiving these bonds would thereafter be responsible for their own retirement and medical expenses. Payroll deductions for Social Security, Medicare "A", federal employee retirement and railroad retirement would cease, and instead of making those payments to the federal government, employers now making these payments – both for themselves as employers and for their employees – would be encouraged to make them instead to their employees as increases in their compensation

The fourth step would be for the Office of Management and Budget and the Congressional Budget Office working together to estimate the average annual revenue for the 30-year period as accurately as they can. This would be a very difficult task, but much of the success of the operation would depend upon its being done with reasonable accuracy.

The fifth step would be to determine the *part* of the debt that could be paid. Average annual income estimated in Step 4 would be one of the actual starting points, but for this scenario total revenue for the year 2002 ($1.853 trillion) will be used. Obligations calculated in Step two would be the other actual starting point, but for this scenario, the $33 trillion calculated by the National Center for Policy Analysis will be used for the obligations. The figure of $33 trillion is used because it is intermediate between the other two calculations of $44 trillion and $21 trillion, and appears to be reasonably accurate. Further, predicating a four percent interest rate and 30 years to pay off the $33 trillion debt, the annual payment would come to$1.89 trillion (Source: Monthly payment Calculator, http://www.interest.com/calculators) which amount is slightly more than the $1.853 trillion of the federal government's total revenue in 2002. Thus, it would be impossible to pay the entire amount the federal government owes since there would be nothing left in any year for defense-related programs, veterans programs, for running the government and for funding "Other" programs.

In this scenario, the federal government would pay the amount that it can pay and default on the rest – about 70 percent of the debt – limiting payments to 30 cents on the dollar uniformly for every aspect of the contractual debt (except that held by the Federal reserve Board). For example, total revenue for the year 2002 according to the Office of Management and Budget ($1.853 trillion) less the $515 billion that was produced by the payroll tax (which would no longer be available once this scenario was in effect), and less the full defense-related and veterans benefits cost, and interest on the approximately $600 billion of debt held by the FRB would leave $838 billion. The debt-related costs for 30 percent of the $33 trillion ($630 billion) subtracted from the $838 billion leaves $208 billion that could be appropriated to run the government and fund "all other" programs.

Reductions in the costs of running the government and of "all other" programs – that is, the rest of the federal government – would have to be severe. Spending for means-tested entitlements and other "mandatory" programs would have to be drastically reduced or eliminated entirely. Federal government employment would have to be cut way back. As soon as possible, spending for national defense and homeland security would have to be sharply reduced as well. All of the measures suggested for cutting costs in Chapter 4, and more, would have to be initiated. Producers (working people), although losing 70 percent of the money they have paid in, would benefit from the elimination of the payroll tax and redirection to them of at least part of the payroll tax employers currently pay to the federal government.

The sixth step, when the decision is made to default, would be to calculate the amount owed to each individual creditor as of a specified date, to issue the new bonds and then begin paying off the debt over the 30-year period.

Each year, the President would submit the annual budget conforming to the limitations described above to the Congress. The Congress could amend the budget as it wished in appropriating funds so long as defense-related and veteran's benefits programs remained fully funded, the funds needed to service the newly issued Treasury bonds were appropriated, and funds for "all other" programs were appropriated within the limits of the remaining estimated revenue. Before signing the appropriations bill, the president would submit it to the Federal Reserve Board (FRB) for final approval of the total amount for each of the four categories. The responsibility of the FRB would be to insure that, above all else, the Treasury makes each of the 360 monthly payments in full and on time to a special fund supervised by the FRB and dedicated exclusively to servicing the debt. The responsibility of the President and the Executive Branch would be to reduce expenditures as necessary to remain within the funds appropriated. Congress would still have authority to raise and lower taxes.

It would have to be expected that actual annual income would usually deviate from the average annual income estimated in step 4 by some amount, and that an adjustment would have to be made each year. In some years, there would be a surplus which would be used by the Treasury to purchase bonds from the FRB. In other years, it may be necessary to borrow money to accommodate a shortage, in which case the Treasury would sell bonds to the FRB. The FRB could refuse to purchase U.S. Treasury securities if a majority of its members felt that the President and Congress had not acted with fiscal responsibility. Once the federal government defaults, it would be difficult to raise money by selling U.S. Treasury securities to the public, and about the only market for years thereafter would be the FRB. Thus, the FRB would be responsible for restraining the Congress from its natural propensity for deficit spending.

The FRB is in a position to act as a watchdog over Congress for two reasons: First, its funding comes from interest on U.S. Treasury securities it owns, and it is thus financially independent of a Congressional appropriation. Second, the penalty Congress would face if the FRB refused to purchase Treasury securities might be another default. It is true that, in retaliation for the Board's declining to purchase securities offered, the president might refuse to re-nominate or Congress might refuse to reconfirm members who had voted for refusing to purchase securities, but neither is likely to try abolishing the FRB since the government would then have no market for its securities at all.

The three virtues of the plan suggested above are: first, that all of those to whom the federal government has obligations of the same caliber would be placed on an equal footing. If the government's debt cannot be paid in full, then holders of Treasury securities and those on the receiving end of binding treaties would suffer losses equal to and along with annuitants. Second, it would eliminate the rapidly increasing obligations for Social Security and Medicare, and provide the means for the federal government to pay a portion of its debts according to its ability. Third, it would go a long way towards getting the federal government entirely out of the insurance business (retirement, medical, deposit, flood, pension benefit guarantees, unemployment, et cetera) where much of the debt has been incurred. The federal government has clearly demonstrated that it is unable to run an insurance business, and completely extricating it from the business would be instrumental in keeping the federal government on a sound fiscal basis in the future.

There is still a question lingering in the minds of many about whether or not the federal government ever belonged in the insurance business. The Tenth Amendment to the Constitution as part of the original Bill of Rights says, "The powers not delegated to the United States by the Constitution, nor prohibited by it to the States, are reserved to the States respectively, or to the people." Those who drafted the Constitution of the United States believed that the enumeration of the specific powers delegated to the federal government in Article I, Section 8, of the Constitution – in which there is no mention of the federal government acting as insurer for anything – combined with the Tenth Amendment would be effective in limiting the powers of the federal government. Their belief proved to be erroneous, first because they did not foresee the broad interpretation that the three branches of the federal government would give to the welfare clause in Article 1, Section 8. The interpretation of this clause (along with a similar interpretation of the interstate commerce clause) is so broad that it has enabled the federal government to undertake almost anything it wishes to do, preempting the States when need be.

Second, drafters also relied on Article I, Section 3 of the Constitution, which stated originally: "The Senate of the United States shall be composed of two Senators from each State *chosen by the Legislature thereof . . .."* [emphasis added] . Amendment XVII, which says, "The Senate of the United States shall be composed of two Senators from each State, *elected by the people thereof . . . .*" [emphasis added] was proposed by Congress and ratified by the States in 1913. Senators chosen by state legislatures would likely not have acceded in the first place to any bill that

38

required such a broad interpretation of the welfare clause as it has been given. Absent the broad interpretation of the welfare clause, the federal government would be exceeding its delegated powers by entering into and being in the insurance business as it now is.

A final thought on this subject is that it would probably be the best course to go back to the gold standard once this process was initiated to insure a balance in future current accounts payments and to stabilize the value of the greenback.

Chapter 4. Downsizing, Cost Cutting and Restructuring.

A. The Size of Government.

1. Employment

One useful method for measuring the size of government is by the number of its employees. In the year 1790, a few years after the United States became a nation, there were 3.9 million people in the 13 states and 39 federal employees, or one federal government employee per 100,000 of population. By the year 1940, the population of the country had swelled to 132.2 million, and the number of federal government employees increased to 700,000 or 530 federal government employees per 100,000 of population. By the year 2000, the population of the U.S.A. had increased to 281.4 million and federal government employment to 2.9 million – counting all federal government civilian employees, full-time and part-time, as well as those employed outside the United States – or 1,031 employees per 100,000 of population. **(Figure d.)**

Besides the 2.9 million federal government employees, there were 4.9 million state government employees and 13.1 million local government employees, for a total of 20.9 million people employed by government. Thus, of the 134 million people employed in the United States in the year 2000, 16 percent of them were employed by government.

2. Cost

Another method for measuring the size of government is by its cost. The year 2002 cost of the federal government (in

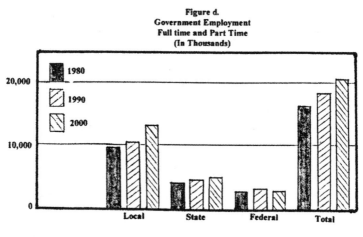

Figure d.
Government Employment
Full time and Part Time
(In Thousands)

Source Bureau of Census, Statistical Abstract

current dollars) was $2.0 trillion, having increased from $42.6 billion in 1950. Because of growth and regular annual inflation, the cost of government is often expressed in terms of percentage of gross domestic product (GDP). The cost of state and local government in the U.S. has grown much faster than the cost of the federal government. The cost of state and local government as a percentage of GDP grew from 5.6 percent in 1950 to 10.1 percent in 2002. Thus, over a span of 49 years, the cost of state and local government nearly doubled as a percentage of GDP. The cost of the federal government grew from 15.6 percent of GDP in 1950 to 19.5 percent in 2002, an increase of 25 percent. During the intervening years, the cost fluctuated within a range at its low of 14.2 percent in 1951 to a high of 23.5 percent in 1983 with the average being about 19 percent.

Many take comfort in the fact that in the year 2002, the cost of the federal government stood at 19.5 percent of the GDP, which is not nearly as high as it was during the World War II years of 1943, 1944, and 1945, when the annual cost of the federal government as a percentage of the GDP was in the forties. However, in the World War II years, the federal government did not have anything approaching the monumental off-the-books debt that it does today. Also, in terms of the whole economy, the cost of state and local government as a percentage of GDP at that time was only a fraction of what it is now.

B. Reasons for Reducing the Size and Cost of Government.

Reducing the costs of government is reason enough in itself for cost cutting and downsizing, but there are two other reasons: The first is to reduce the volume and complexity of laws and regulations, and the second is to improve the capability of American industry and agriculture for competing in international trade.

1. Law and Regulation, Volume and Complexity.

The individual American citizen has passively and gradually given up more and more authority and freedom to government. One gauge of how much has been given up is the volume of laws and regulations extant today. Legislators have relentlessly enacted more and more laws over the years, and government officials have written more and more regulations. The effect of many of these new laws and regulations is to take authority away from the individual and give it to government. When the government takes authority (and freedom), the individuals governed no longer have it. Authority is like money in that respect. The encroachment was so slow that we hardly noticed it was happening. Some laws and regulations are necessary, of course, but the way our current governments are set up, more are added regularly (rarely rescinded) to a growing mass of statutes, ordinances and regulations. Naturally, this is not an argument for no government. Everyone recognizes that government and only government can perform certain functions, such as the defense of the country. Without government, we would have anarchy. On the other hand, we have seen the adverse effects of big government on the freedoms of individuals in the former USSR, China, and in other countries. We have also seen the adverse effects big government can have on free enterprise.

Some people want the government to take yet more responsibility and do not mind the loss of their individual authority and freedom that goes with it. These people are willing to make the trade. They are like young children comfortable with their parents having nearly all of the responsibility for their welfare and the authority over them. However, when young children become teenagers, they usually rebel at this situation because they want more freedom and are willing to accept (sometimes reluctantly) the responsibility that goes with the freedom. Some adults never reach the teenage level of maturity. For them, government becomes a surrogate parent.

Official federal law is contained in the Statutes at Large which are difficult to use because they are arranged in chronological order by year of enactment. To simplify finding the law, the general and permanent statutes have been compiled into the United States Code, where the law is arranged and codified by subject. The Code consists of 27 volumes, totaling about 35,000 pages, plus two volumes of tables and a seven-volume index to aid in its use. Knowing the wording of statutes is not enough; one must know how the courts have construed the statutes. For this, one must refer to either the U.S. Code Annotated or the Federal Code Annotated. The United States Code Annotated, which includes the combined federal laws, regulations, and judicial decisions (necessary to understand and apply federal law), is in 247 volumes with about 194,000 pages updated with cumulative pocket parts and. supplemental pamphlets.

Besides the laws enacted by Congress, there are numerous federal proclamations, orders, regulations, notices, and other documents that are legally binding. These are included in the Federal Register (FR), which is published daily. One year of the Federal Register takes up about six shelves in a legal library. Because the mass of material appearing in the FR is in chronological order and difficult to use, most of its contents are arranged by subject in the Code of Federal Regulations, of some 130,000 pages. Although the FR and the CFR are the primary official sources, many agencies, such as the Internal Revenue Service, Federal Communications Commission, and Federal Power Commission, issue their own texts, rules, regulations, decisions, and annual reports.

States have their own codes or compilation of their laws, as well as other sources of legal information similar to those of the federal government. Virginia, for example, has the Virginia Code Annotated of 13 volumes and about 16,000 pages. Municipalities also have their own codes of laws. For example, the Alexandria, Virginia, code is contained in two volumes totaling about 2,600 pages.

Legislation is only part of the law. The other part is case law. These are cases adjudicated by appellate courts where judges have construed and interpreted legislation and regulations. These cases, through the doctrine of *stare decisis,* also become law since judges are committed (usually) to adjudicate their cases in accordance with earlier cases that are the same or similar. Case law is even more voluminous than legislative law.

Nobody, including legislators, lawyers and judge – and certainly not the average citizen – can know all that there is in this massive body of federal, state, and local law and cases. For one thing, the law is constantly being added to and changed by federal, state, and local legislative organizations and is constantly being construed by the courts and government agencies. Fortunately, only some of it applies to any particular individual, but to know with any degree of certainty what the law really is that *does* apply to a particular individual may require the services of a skilled legal researcher working industriously for as much as a couple of days using a roomful of legal publications. Ultimately, a judge may have to decide what the law really is. Nevertheless, we are presumed by the courts to know the law. What else can they do?

Not only is there such a large body of law and regulation, but some of the law is so complex that it defies comprehension. The Internal Revenue Service cannot implement a few sections of the tax law that has been enacted by Congress because it is impossible to understand them. The legislation gets that way after each of the 535 Senators and Congressmen has had a chance to include his own individual input. Just getting an agreement on something is the main thing for most legislators. How difficult and costly the law will be to understand, comply with and administer appears to be a relatively inconsequential matter. Compromise is what they seek. If they can just get that, they gather together, clap one another on the back and happily drink champagne.

2. Increase Competitiveness in
International Trade.

Trade competition among the nations of the world has been ongoing since the beginning of recorded history, but it has received renewed emphasis in the United States now that the government has embraced free international trade as a policy. The needs for trade are similar to those needed for a cold war or a hot war. Needed to be competitive are efficient and creative industrial management; modern efficient manufacturing plants; suitable infrastructure; a well-motivated, healthy, energetic, educated workforce; and lastly, low overhead costs.

The question of U.S. competitiveness is of more immediate concern now more than ever before because other nations which have been traditionally agricultural, such as China, India, Mexico, Brazil, and some of the southeast Asian countries are beginning to develop industrially. With an abundant low-cost labor force – which in many instances is also healthy, energetic, well motivated, and well educated – these nations have a great competitive advantage, particularly when their industries are efficiently and creatively managed, when there is a suitable infrastructure, and when the cost of government is low. The significant adverse international trade balance that the United States experiences nearly every month is indicative that the nation is not now competing effectively.

The United States economy should be able to compete in a climate of free trade because we are well situated with respect to three of the four necessary elements of production; namely, capital, materials and labor. We are surfeited with overhead, the fourth element. We need to look for potential competitive advantage among all four.

The United States is blessed with a wealth of capital at this time, but capital is mobile and in demand worldwide. A competitive advantage is not likely to be realized on capital because, to attract

46

capital, enterprises in the United States will have to pay the going rate that capital can command elsewhere in the world, risks being equal. Capital will move across international borders to wherever it can realize the highest return at the same level of risk. We have restrictions –although not very effective ones – on the movement of people (labor) across international borders, but we do not have and can hardly have effective restrictions on the international movement of capital. Therefore, significant reductions in capital costs cannot be reasonably expected as a means of realizing competitive advantage.

Materials are essential. Many wars have been fought over the possession and control of material resources. No products and few services can be produced without them, but there cannot be any reasonable expectation of any significant price reductions over the long haul in commodities such as grain, energy products, metals, fibers, and lumber. There is a world market for most commodities which are fungible and are priced uniformly throughout the world (costs of insurance, brokering, financing, and transportation excepted). To the contrary, not only can reductions in the price of commodities not be reasonably expected in the future, but increasing demand from a growing world population and the industrialization of heretofore underdeveloped countries can be expected to create an upward pressure on the price of commodities. Therefore, in the end, cost-cutting to achieve a competitive advantage cannot be expected in this area.

Labor is the element that holds the greatest potential for cost reduction of the four. Although impossible to measure precisely, the great preponderance of the value in any service or product is labor. It is difficult to overestimate its value. The value of services is almost entirely that of labor, and there is often more labor value in products than meets the eye. Take, for example the Mid-western wheat farmer. The land he farms is flat, so he is able to prepare the soil, plant, fertilize, and reap with a tractor, a gang

47

plow, and other large machinery. Thus, by virtue of the quality of the land and availability of machinery, the wheat farmer can produce a large quantity of grain for each unit of his own labor.

The wheat farmer's plow and the tractor are certainly factors contributing to the value of the farmer's product, but the value in both the plow and the tractor is mostly that of the labor that fabricated them. However, the value of his plow and tractor is not entirely labor, because their component parts have value. The parts themselves were fabricated by labor from materials — in this case, mostly steel. The steel was produced by labor from iron ore. Again, although most of the value of the steel is in the labor that went into making it, some of the value was in the iron ore the steel was made from, but the ore did not have much value until it was dug from the ground and transported by labor to a furnace and a mill over highways, railroads, and bridges in vehicles all constructed by labor. Some of the steel's value was also in the energy (coke) and chemicals (limestone) used in making it, but these also were of little value until mined and transported by labor.

The American work force is well motivated and is perhaps one of the hardest working peoples in the world. They are healthy, energetic, and well educated, although indications are that the level of education required to meet the requirements of industry has begun to decline. At the time of this writing, the rate of unemployment in the United States is less than six percent. Americans work longer hours than workers in other industrialized nations. Americans currently are said to be paid less than workers in the other two dozen or so industrialized countries. The operative word in the sentence is "industrialized." It is certainly true that American labor, especially unskilled labor, is paid vastly more than labor in the developing countries of the world. It is for this reason that the label on so many items one picks up in a store says "Made in China."

When most people think about the cost of labor, they think exclusively about the wages of lower level unskilled and semiskilled employees in the fields or on the factory floor. Management of businesses, although labor of a different type, is still labor, and the salaries, bonuses, and perquisites of senior executives in large corporations are often obscenely high. Undoubtedly, this situation results from the fact that, many times, members of the board of directors of the corporation are nominated to these lucrative positions by the CEO or other prominent executives in the company. When the CEO suggests high rates of remuneration for himself and his subordinates, these board members are not likely to disagree. Although only a small part of the total labor cost, this is an area where substantial economies could be realized.

The fourth element, overhead, is the other area where significant cost reductions can be made. It was perhaps 15 or 20 years ago that American industries, acting out of necessity, began downsizing and applying the principles of quality improvement to cut costs, including their overhead costs. In doing this, they were quick to take advantage of rapidly developing electronic technology and the Internet to improve the efficiency of their operations. This process is well along now. Both American industry and agriculture have come a long way towards recapturing a once-threatened competitive position in world trade.

What we do *not* have is low-cost government (federal, state, and local) which is part of the nation's overhead. It holds great potential for cost reduction. Although Al Gore when he was vice president, had some success in effecting reductions in the number of federal government employees, these were mostly reductions in the Department of Defense after the cold war ended. No serious effort has ever been made to drastically downsize the rest of the federal government and reduce its cost. State and local governments have been growing rapidly and steadily, as indicated in section B.1. above. Taxes levied to support swollen governments add significantly to the cost of goods and services and diminish competitiveness. In a world of free international trade competition, the cost of government in the United States will hang like an albatross around the neck of American labor and the economy.

Two questions are currently subject of heated discussion: First, is international free trade a worthy concept. Second, if it is, what can the federal government do to increase global competitiveness of producers in the United States?

Free trade is probably accepted by the majority of the people in the world who think about trade at all as an economic benefit to the world as a whole because of the principle of comparative advantage. The principle of comparative advantage works like this: if producers in the United States can make computers more efficiently than they can in China, but the Chinese can make shirts more efficiently than we can make them in the United States, then the most efficient thing to do for both countries is for the United States to make computers for both the U.S. and China, and for China to do the same for shirts. Then trade. However, just because the effect of the principle of comparative advantage is likely to provide economic benefits for the world as a whole, this does not mean that all peoples will benefit equally or, indeed, that some peoples will benefit at all. Some will be injured. Free trade has a leveling effect on living standards. Living standards of developing countries tend to increase. Living standards of developed countries may also increase, but they may also stay the same or decrease.

Opponents of free trade are protectionists. Their wish is to protect domestic industries through the use of government imposed tariffs, import quotas, guaranteed price programs and the like. Protectionists have basically three arguments in support of their position, the most common of which is that free trade will mean a loss of jobs. Some of this country's manufacturing industries – the textile industry and the jobs in those industries as a case in point

– have already been largely picked up and moved offshore. Now, many clerical and technical jobs in the service industries are being outsourced to other countries via the Internet. What will happen to American workers who would have filled these jobs? It may be a repetition of what happened when the integrated steel industry foundered in the late 70's and early 80's. Workers will retire if they are old enough and have enough service with their company to do so; they will become unemployed; or they will find other jobs, many of them lower-paying jobs such as driving taxicabs or stocking grocery store shelves. Some displaced workers will learn new skills and get better jobs. The slick answer often given to the loss of technical jobs now being outsourced is that displaced American workers will find higher-level, higher-paying jobs that will be created. Perhaps, but there is no assurance of that.

It is clear that protectionist measures can save some jobs in selected special interest industries, What is not clear are the unintended adverse consequences of these self-same measures which are of two kinds. First, jobs are often lost in industries related to the protected special interest industry, although whether more or less jobs are lost than are saved is difficult to ascertain. The other certain unintended adverse consequence is higher taxes, higher prices or both for taxpayers and consumers.

Another argument against free international trade with far less merit is the infant industries argument. The argument here is that newly-formed industries need protection by way of tariffs and import quotas until they can get on their feet and compete with the same industries in foreign countries that have already been developed and are ongoing. The problem with this argument is that, once the industry gets protection, it need not compete anymore, often never does become competitive on the world market, and remains dependent upon a government subsidy for its existence. The sugar production industry in the United States is a good example.

The argument protectionists have with the most merit is that the nation's ability to defend itself militarily will be impaired. If we should have to go to war, could we reasonably expect the Chinese to manufacture uniforms for our soldiers? Or could we expect the Koreans to provide the steel we need? Could the United States itself begin manufacturing, on short notice, the quantities of materiel that would be needed in case war broke out?

Three elements are required for the production of war materiel: They are: materials (Including energy, which is usually in the basic form of coal, oil, gas, or uranium,), capital (including manufacturing plants and infrastructure), and labor. We can and do stockpile materials needed for war production, but the quantities and kinds of materials in the stockpile may not be what is needed to produce modern weapons. We can and have mothballed plants for manufacturing war materiel that could be reopened quickly, although mothballed plants in today's market soon become obsolescent. The United States has plenty of labor, but we cannot stockpile the people skills required to operate the mothballed plants. Those skills are wasting assets soon lost and not quickly or easily replaced.

Can the United States afford to protect every domestic industry that makes a claim to being an essential war industry? Probably not. Almost any industry can make a fairly reasoned claim to being an essential war industry. At one time the wooden clothespin manufacturing industry in Maine claimed to be one. Like it or not, the United States does now and in time of war would have to rely, to some extent at least, on other countries to provide needed war materiel.

There is another aspect of protectionism that needs to be examined, and that is on what basis are decisions made to impose tariffs, import quotas, guaranteed prices and the like? There are some instances where protectionist measures are genuinely warranted. One is tariffs or import quotas to prevent industries

52

in other countries from dumping their products in this country at prices below their production costs. Another is to compensate domestic manufacturers for costs incurred for implementing environmental regulations, the like of which manufacturers in other countries are not subject. Here again, almost any industry can make some kind of an argument on these bases.

Too often, however, the basis is really political. If a politician concludes that the success of his next election depends upon getting more votes in the state of Pennsylvania where many steelworkers reside, he may place restrictions on the importation of low-priced foreign-produced steel. This allows for increases in the price of domestic steel, may result in an increase in domestic production and an increase in the number of workers employed by the steel industry in Pennsylvania. Grateful workers could be expected to vote in the next election for their benefactor. For a worker living in the state of Michigan where many automobiles are manufactured, this may not be such great news. As the price of steel, a basic material in the manufacture of automobiles goes up, the price of automobiles goes up, fewer are sold, and the auto worker may lose his job.

Sugar sells for about six cents a pound in the world market. That price represents capitalism at work. However, sugar producers in the United States get about twenty cents a pound for their sugar. That price represents the politically motivated federal government price support programs at work. These programs are in effect because sugar producers are large contributors to the political campaigns of incumbent federal legislators seeking reelection. When the government supports the sugar at twenty cents a pound, domestic confectioners, food processors and, ultimately, the American consumer pay the extra fourteen cents a pound in the way of higher prices for candy and other processed food products. There are dozens of subsidy programs in existence similar to the sugar programs. Most of them cost us dearly.

In summary, there are two conclusions that may be fairly drawn from the foregoing: The first is that free trade, on balance, is better than protectionism. Second, the federal government can do two things to increase the global competitiveness of producers in the United States. Besides shrinking the size and cost of government (overhead), it can get out of the way by eliminating politically motivated subsidies of all kinds so that the capitalistic system can work at setting prices through the interaction of supply and demand.

C. Guidance.

1. Philosophy of Government.

Thomas Jefferson described good government this way: [*one*] . . . *which shall restrain men from injuring one another, which shall leave them otherwise free to regulate their own pursuits of industry and improvement, and shall not take from the mouth of labor the bread it has earned.*"

This is the philosophy of government to which conservatives subscribe and the Republican Party purports to subscribe by its words, but one which it often does not practice. Liberals and the Democratic Party, on the other hand, openly and notoriously subscribe to the philosophy that government – and particularly the federal government – rightfully should play a far more prominent and intimate role in our lives than it now does, and they do pursue that philosophy in practice.

If we were to adopt the current philosophy of many enlightened industries, we would probably reach agreement on the following guidance in selecting functions to be performed by government:

Government at any level should not perform any function that can be performed at a lower level of government, or by families, or by individuals, thus insuring that responsibility for the maximum number of functions (and the authority to go with them) resides at the lowest level of government, or with the family and the individual.

2. Vision of Government

As a first step towards accomplishing any change, some vision should be involved in deciding what the Nation (in the case of the national government) wants to be in 50 years, what goals it wishes to achieve along the way, and what principles will be followed in reaching them. Otherwise, we could end up worse off than we are now. The challenges are to recognize the need for changes on our part, reluctant as we may be to do so, and to adapt to those needs in logical and reasonable ways, although the solutions at times may be different and even radically different from those to which we have grown accustomed. The vision should be debated, agreed upon, and set down in writing.

A vision of the United States might be: A nation that wishes to maintain the integrity of its present borders and the security of its citizens, has no hostile designs on the territory of other nations and wishes to remain as a nation that is militarily and economically strong and a good neighbor to other nations, with a government that is least intrusive into the lives of its citizens, is empowered by the people it governs, and furthers the right of the people to life, liberty, and the pursuit of happiness.

3. Goals

The need for goals is well illustrated by the following exchange between Alice and the Cheshire-cat from the Lewis Carroll book, *Alice in Wonderland*:

Alice: *Would you tell me, please, which way I ought to go from here?*

Cat : *That depends a good deal on where you want to go to.*

Alice*: I don't much care where,*

Cat: *Then it doesn't matter which way you go.*

The basic goal for the United States is well stated in the Declaration of Independence:

We hold these Truths to be self-evident, that all Men are ... endowed by their Creator with certain unalienable Rights, that among these are Life, Liberty, and the Pursuit of Happiness --

The federal government's twin primary goals at this time are to bolster the nation's economy and to make life safer for American citizens by wiping out terrorism and terrorist organizations in the world, to include dealing with the countries of Iraq, North Korea, and Iran, any of which have the resources and the apparent will to conspire with terrorist organizations that endanger the citizens of this country. Beyond that, we do not now seem to have a comprehensive set of specific national goals and guidelines that are based on principles, accepted nationally, and widely publicized. The closest that the nation comes to this now is the adoption of platforms by political parties during presidential campaigns. Candidates discuss the planks in their party's platform, herald them during the campaign and then largely ignore them after the campaign is over. Until the next campaign, whatever national goals that there are appear to be determined rather cynically on the basis of temporary political expediency; i.e., what is most likely to get individual politicians reelected.

Without goals, the government in the past has led the nation into a number of international misadventures involving no particular national interest. The most egregious of these gambits was the disastrous war with Viet Nam. On the other hand, the nation had a specific interest in defending Kuwait against Iraqi aggression: oil. Later on, Kosovo, another misadventure not so costly in lives and treasure, demonstrated that the government still had not learned its lesson. Priding itself on being the world's only remaining superpower, one might say that the government has led the nation into becoming an international Don Quixote jousting with windmills all over the world, or a Sir Galahad on quest, sometimes meddling in the internal affairs of other nations – the self-appointed police officer of the planet.

4. Rules and Principles

With regard to downsizing and streamlining, the government should subscribe to rules and principles. Basically, these rules may be that governments should:

a. See to it that all authorities and responsibilities reside at the very lowest level in the nation's social structure where they can be performed. This would mean that many of the authorities now exercised by government at all levels would be returned to the individual and the family. Many now exercised by the federal government would be returned to the States, etc.

b. Be oriented for responding to the needs and desires of the people. The people do the work, create the value, and pay the taxes; the people are the customers. Too often, politicians seem to feel that political party chiefs, special interest groups, political action committees, and those, in general, who put up the large sums of money usually required to be elected to public office today, are the customers. They are not.

c. Mind their own business and refrain from meddling in the internal affairs of other nations.

d. Live within their means.

e. Honor their legal contracts and pay their lawful debts. (For the federal government and some state and municipal governments, this will not be an easy (or even possible) task at the time of this writing and in the future.)

f. Accept natural law.

g. Recognize that the majority rules.

h. Encourage those in the majority *and* the minorities to strive to be both tolerant and tolerable. In the words of the American actress Katherine Hepburn, "We have to put up with one another." We live in a multi-cultural, multi-ethnic, multi-racial, multi-religious society, and we must get along. There is no viable alternative.

i. Refrain from trying to protect the individual from himself in all areas including drinking, smoking, eating, using drugs, and gambling.

5. Motto.

Every citizen should have as his motto that he does not want government subsidies of any kind and does not want others to have any either.

6. Oath of Office.

Every politician should take the following oath or affirmation before beginning the duties of his elected office:
"I do solemnly swear (or affirm) that I will
faithfully perform the duties of my office, will

to the best of my ability preserve, protect, and defend the Constitution of the United States, and will limit my official actions to those intended to benefit the majority of my constituents, with those actions excepted that are intended to provide immediate emergency relief for victims of war, terrorism, and forces of nature."

D. Downsize and Cost-Cut the Executive Branch.

A beginning would be made towards uncovering organizations and functions in which the federal government is unnecessarily involved if the Congress began sun-setting all federal legislation and regulations over a ten-year period. For example, in the year 2004, review all legislation enacted and regulations implemented in years ending in the number four. At the end of ten years, all previously-enacted legislation and previously implemented regulations would have been reviewed. All legislation not reenacted and all regulations not reimplemented in the review year would be automatically repealed. That would be helpful, but that alone is not enough. Until the Executive Branch of the federal government is placed on a very tight budget and forced to root out inappropriate and unaffordable organizations and functions itself, cost reductions will never approach the potential. Here are some examples of possible reductions or eliminations:

1. Legalize Controlled Substances

The manufacture, sale, transportation, importation or exportation of intoxicating liquors was prohibited by the Eighteenth Amendment to the U.S. Constitution, which was proposed by Congress in 1918, ratified by the States in 1919, and put into effect in 1920. Bootlegging, smuggling, killing, and gang warfare ran rampant in the following thirteen years until the Eighteenth Amendment was repealed by the Twenty-first Amendment in 1933. In those13 years of Prohibition, the federal government learned its lesson and gave up on trying to protect the American people from themselves – temporarily. Thirty-seven years later, the federal government had forgotten the lesson it had learned and enacted the Controlled Substances Act, Title II of the Comprehensive Abuse Prevention and Control Act of 1970, which is the legal foundation for the government efforts to control the illicit manufacture and distribution of a wide variety of narcotics, stimulants, depressants, hallucinogens and anabolic steroids. (Unlike with Prohibition, no constitutional amendment was required. In the interim years between 1918 and 1970, the interpretation of the welfare and interstate commerce clauses of the U.S. Constitution had been so broadened that the federal government could engage in the same kind of activities as they did during Prohibition with only the enactment of simple legislation.) Now, we find ourselves in a situation similar to the Prohibition era with bootlegging, smuggling, killing, gang warfare, and the prisons bulging with (largely) convicted drug dealers and users.

Besides trying to interdict the traffic of illicit drugs into and within the United States, the Drug Enforcement Administration of the federal government has several programs extant for trying to control or eliminate the production of such drugs in several foreign countries. These are Sisyphean tasks because, as the DEA goes busily about "busting" dealers and destroying large quantities of drugs and drug-making materials, more drugs, more materials, and more dealers keep coming in a steady stream. The DEA is engaged in an uphill struggle at great cost to control supply, a struggle which can never be won.

Several other countries have suggested an approach to the problem that is 180 degrees different from the one currently being employed in the United States; that is, by legally satisfying the demand for (what are now) illicit drugs instead of trying to curtail the supply. The Netherlands successfully employs a solution such as this by providing a plentiful supply of drugs that are cheap and of standard strength and purity. Cannot the American people be trusted to control their own behavior? Does the federal government have to do it for us? When Prohibition was repealed in 1933, there were many who thought we would become a nation of drunks. It didn't happen. The only reason we have illicit drug traffic in the United States today is because there are big profits to be made in it, and big profits can be made in it only because suppliers have to take big risks. Satisfying the demand legally by selling the drugs in drug stores would cost nothing at all and, indeed, the federal government might extract a little tax money from the legalized trade. The illicit drug trade would come to a screeching halt just like the illicit liquor trade did in 1933.

Cocaine, for example is not much different than caffeine. Originally, the Coca-Cola soft drink contained both cocaine and caffeine as stimulants. When cocaine was banned, caffeine was continued with much the same stimulative effect. People who are addicted to caffeine or nicotine and many of those addicted to alcohol lead normal, productive lives despite their addictions. Could not users of marijuana or cocaine still lead normal, productive lives despite their addiction if they did not have to pay high prices for their supply? Many, if not most, of the deaths and illnesses that result from the use of drugs stem from the fact that these drugs obtained illicitly vary greatly in strength and purity. Users never know exactly what they are getting. If aspirin were not compounded and sold in tablets of standard strength and purity, thousands of people would get sick from overdosing and some would die from aspirin poisoning. There are cost savings of trillions of dollars to be had here by a simple reorientation in the approach to the problem.

2. Control Immigration.

Equally large cost saving could be realized by implementing suggestions regarding immigration described in Chapter 7.

3. Reform the Penal System.

Reformation of the Penal system as described in Chapter 8 would go far to cutting the cost of the federal government.

4. Other

a. Repeal minimum wage and (in localities) living wage legislation. This would cut the cost of labor and increase the number of jobs available for unskilled and low skilled workers.

b. Repeal the Americans with Disabilities Act. This was compassion legislation that has turned out to be expensive and wasteful.

c. Terminate mandates, grants and payments of all kinds to state and local governments and repeal the underlying legislation. If the functions subject of mandate and grants can best be performed by state or local government, they should either perform them and fund them themselves or the functions should not be performed at all.

d. Terminate subsidy payments to foreign countries except those payments required to honor binding treaty obligations. Set timetables for terminating such subsidies and, to the extent possible, unilaterally abrogating treaties or sections of treaties requiring them.

e. Terminate subsidies of all kinds to all groups in the U.S., including manufacturers and farmers, and repeal underlying legislation.

f. Terminate subsidies to Amtrac, which should be self sustaining and receive no governmental aid. If that is not possible, the nation should forego national passenger rail service.

g. Privatize air traffic control which should be provided by an association of airline companies, and abolish this function of the Federal Aviation Administration.

h. Terminate all federal contributions for unemployment insurance which should be provided by private insurance companies, by the States or not at all.

i. Abolish the Bureau of Indian Affairs. Native Americans would be better served by abrogating the Indian treaties, returning their properties and lands to them to manage themselves, albeit under the laws of the jurisdictions in which the properties and lands are situate.

j. Abolish the National Oceanic and Atmospheric Administration. The services it now provides should be provided by private organizations.

k. Terminate all connections to government-sponsored enterprises, explicit and implicit, and publicly disavow sponsorship of such enterprises as the Federal National Mortgage Association, the Federal Home Mortgage Association, the Federal Home Loan Bank System, and similar organizations.

l. Privatize the Postal Service, retaining only certain regulatory powers.

m. Get out of the loan and loan guarantee business.

E. Reorganize and Downsize Congress.

Congress, the federal legislative body, is bicameral. It has 535 members and thousands of staff. It has 36 standing committees, four special and select committees, four joint committees, and 159 subcommittees. Many of these committees and subcommittees have overlapping responsibilities, a condition which complicates the legislative process. Its operation costs about $3.5 billion a year. All of this just to make federal law and oversee its execution. It is a ponderous, cumbersome body that spends a good deal of its time every year on trivial matters and internecine struggles. It is so large that it gets in its own way in trying to accomplish anything, and its products are frequently very poor. Although it takes several extended vacations each year, it meets essentially all year round. It meets for so long because it has involved itself in almost any matter that you can think of. Solons vie to get legislation on the calendar or, even better, enacted into law. They feel that doing so is a measure of their worth and helpful in getting reelected. Not only does Congress produce too much legislation, but the legislation is all-too-frequently incomprehensible to the layman and, at times, even to the government agency charged with its implementation. Legislators cannot possibly read all of the legislation that they enact, and they commonly vote on final bills without having read them in their entirety or at all.

Originally, most governmental power was vested in the States. The federal government's phenomenal usurpation of authority from the States, local governments and individuals began in earnest with the New Deal programs of Franklin D. Roosevelt, elected president in 1932. It continued with the so-called "Warren Court" (1953-1969) and the "Burger Court" (1969-1986) when Earl Warren and Warren Burger were the Chief Justices. During these periods, the Supreme Court's interpretation of the interstate commerce and welfare clauses of the Constitution was such that the federal government had authority to preempt State's rights in anything remotely connected with either interstate commerce or the welfare of the people and the nation. Amendment XVI to the U.S. Constitution, ratified by the States in 1913, gave the federal government the right to tax the incomes of individuals. This legislation, together with Social Security and Medicare legislation, provides the means by which the federal government funds the extensive programs it has enacted into law.

The drafters of the U.S. Constitution originally contemplated a Congress with a single wing having proportional representation by state according to population, but ratification of the Constitution by the required nine of the original thirteen states was by no means a sure thing. Small states like Delaware were concerned that they would not have an adequate voice in Congress because of their small populations. Hence, to court the approval of the smaller states, a Senate wing was added with two senators from each State, regardless of the State's population.

Notice the resemblance between the bicameral Congress and the British parliament, with the Senate being comparable to the House of Lords and the House of Representatives being comparable to the House of Commons. For centuries, a king or a queen ruled the British Empire but in the year 1215, English nobles forced the king to sign the Magna Carta which guaranteed them and the church privileges against the monarchy and assured jury trials. After that time, the British Empire was ruled by the monarch and the nobles until Parliament evolved with a House of Lords, comprised of the lords who had formerly ruled the empire, and the House of Commons, which developed in the late thirteenth and early fourteenth centuries giving the common people a voice in government for the first time including the power to raise taxes. Over time, the House of Commons came to dominate. Thus, the bicameral legislature was born. Are we in that situation today? Must we continue to cede to our plutocracy – the equivalent of the British nobility -- a separate wing in Congress? Would not a unicameral legislature be more workable and more efficient? Unicameral legislatures are not new. The State of Nebraska has one that appears to work well.

The United States cannot afford to replace our present bicameral national legislature with just any organization. It will have to be replaced with an organization that has been tried and has stood up as a viable and workable organization over time in a similar environment. Fortunately, such an organization exists. It is one with which we are all familiar — the corporate board of directors. A National Board of Directors would be more effective, more efficient, less cumbersome, and less costly to operate than bicameral legislative bodies like the Congress, and would better represent the people of the nation. Corporations have used boards of directors with reasonable success as a form of policy making body for many years.

Each state would have an equal number of representatives on the Board; that is, each state would have one representative, so that 50 of them would make up the National Board of Directors. Terms of office would be for four years. The Board would elect a chairperson from volunteers within its own ranks. The Board would elect the members of the Executive Council from those within its own ranks who volunteer for the service. The Board would agree upon the number of Council members, but the number should not be greater than nine. The Executive Council would elect its own chairperson by majority vote from those within its own ranks who volunteered for the job. The Council would conduct investigations, hold hearings, draft legislation, and present it to the Board for enactment. The Council would make reports to the Board when it was in session and receive regular reports from the president and department heads on the operations of the Executive Branch throughout the year.

The Board would also select a president of the United States (for a term of four years or until removed by the Board) either from within its own ranks or from outside. An individual would be selected who had demonstrated management skills and who had some military background. The home state of the individual elected as president (if a member of the Board were elected as president) would elect a substitute member for the Board in accordance with the electoral process.

The Board would only meet two or three times a year for a month or so at a time. At those times, among other things, the Board would receive reports from the Board's Executive Council and the president. Voting would be proportional according to the number of registered voters in each state. The state with the smallest number of registered voters would have one vote. Other states would have proportionately more votes according to number of registered voters, with the number of votes rounded to the nearest whole number. It would be the responsibility of the Board to enact legislation and determine policy much as Congress does today. One of the first responsibilities would be to sunset-review all existing federal legislation over a ten-year period with a view to repealing it, modifying it, or reenacting it. All legislation reviewed and not specifically reenacted, either in its existing form or as modified, would be automatically repealed.

The desirable feature of such an organization is that it can be and should be tried at local and state levels before it is tried at the national level. In fact, the concept is in effect at some local levels in part, at least, at this time. The City of Alexandria, Virginia, for one, has a city council that works very well and is the equivalent at the local level of a National Council. However, a new electoral system would be needed before legislative bodies – as they are presently constituted – could be converted, because those elected by the present electoral system would not have an incentive to accomplish such a conversion. A new electoral system is discussed in Part III.

F. Downsize the Federal Judicial System.

The federal judicial system costs about $4 billion a year to operate. The primary purpose of a judicial system is to settle civil disputes and punish criminals quickly, fairly, with finality and at a reasonable cost. The present judicial system has none of these characteristics. The judicial system in this country has been honed to the point where it offers exquisite justice, but it fails utterly in its primary purpose.

Over the years, it has grown into a pettifogging monster with voluminous procedural rules and precedents which cause it to be more likely that the relative skills of the opposing attorneys are more important to the outcome of the case than are its merits. Thus, wealthier litigants who can afford to hire better lawyers improve their chances of winning a case over a opponent less well-endowed financially. This country is a nation of litigators. With such a heavy caseload, the ponderous and intricate rules of civil and criminal procedures assure lengthy delays in completing cases. The extensive and complex rules lend themselves to attorneys for wealthier litigants dragging cases out excessively through legal maneuvering, thus financially exhausting the other party who may be less wealthy or just plain poor. Some years ago a court of appeals chided a District Court judge in the District of Columbia for not hearing a case for ten years. Criminals sometimes sit on death row for years while their convictions are being appealed at various levels. Some die of natural causes or old age before their appeals are exhausted

.

1. Limit Appeals.

The cost of the Nation's judicial system can be dramatically reduced with little reduction in the quality of the results by simply not allowing appeals except for alleged violations of the

Constitution. Litigants would take their case to the court of proper jurisdiction, give it their best shot, accept the result, put the case behind them, and go on with their lives. Since almost all of case law is written by appellate courts, that part of the huge body of law we have would not be enlarged and would eventually become irrelevant.

The outcome of any legal case in one sense, whether civil or criminal, is the same no matter what. The winning party believes the decision is fair and just, and the losing party believes it is unfair. What's fair? What one person would call fair may very well not be fair at all to another. When a baseball umpire announces "Fair ball," he does that in accordance with a strict rule. If the ball is not hit outside the first or third base lines, it is a fair ball. Most of the time, in leading our daily lives, there are no such cut-and-dried rules by which to judge fairness. Most of us judge fairness by what we have been taught by our parents or teachers to be fair or by some standard, like the Golden Rule, subject to interpretation.

If the decision of the trial court is appealed and reversed, then the parties reverse their views about the fairness of the outcome. In the meantime, much time has elapsed and much money has been spent by the litigants on attorney fees and court costs. Appellate courts review decisions of lower courts for the purpose of deciding whether or not procedures were followed properly and whether or not pertinent law was applied correctly. If the appellate court reverses the lower court because it decides procedures were not properly followed or that pertinent law was not applied correctly, are we sure that they were not? Perhaps, the appellate court was wrong? To resolve this question, society and the legal system have simply postulated that the appellate court is always correct -- that is, unless the case is appealed to a still higher court that decides differently.

Could we not just as well postulate that the trial court followed procedures and applied the law correctly in the first place and forget the appeals? If we did that, once the gavel came down in the trial court, the case would be over, and the litigants – whether they believed the outcome to be fair or unfair – could get on with their lives. After all, there cannot be any real assurance that the appellate court is correct when it differs from the trial court. If one reviews opinions of the United States Supreme Court, it often appears that the dissenting opinion(s) make more sense than the majority opinion. Another problem is, who can take advantage of avenues of appeals? With some exceptions, such as when a law firm can be interested in taking the case on a contingency or on a pro bono basis, or when an organization like the American Civil Liberties Union agrees to take the case at no charge, only those who have deep pockets can afford it. The financial resources of most litigants are exhausted by the time -- or, perhaps, even before -- they get the decision from an appeals court. Think of the effort, time, money and disruption to the lives of the litigants that would be saved if appeals were limited.

Such a restriction on appeals should be easy for the American people to accept because in the fine print of many contracts that individuals enter into today, there is provision for binding arbitration. The American people sign such contracts regularly and willingly or, perhaps, unknowingly. Witness credit card contracts. Usually, the company that the individual is contracting with has much more to say about who the arbitrator will be than does the individual, which gives the company a decided advantage in reaching an outcome favorable to the company. In a trial court of law, the two sides are more likely to be treated equally.

2. No-Fault Insurance.

Beyond disallowing appeals, there are four other measures than can be taken to lighten the caseload on the nation's courts. The first of these is to legislate no-fault automobile liability insurance. No-fault insurance is nothing new. It has been discussed and debated for a long time, and some states have tried it. The way it is now in most states, when there is an automobile accident, the injured party tries to reach an out-of-court settlement with the other party. Failing that, the injured party sues the other party involved in the accident for money damages to cover the cost of whatever injuries or losses were incurred or can be expected to be incurred due to the accident. Because parties often do not succeed in reaching a settlement themselves, litigation resulting from automobile accidents constitutes a major part of the civil caseload for courts.

Under no-fault insurance, instead of trying to settle with or by suing the other party involved in an automobile accident, both parties would look to their own insurance companies to recover the costs of their injuries, damages and losses. One might speculate that there would be an increase in the amount of litigation of another sort; i.e., the injured party, unable to reach a settlement with his own insurance company, sues his own company. Although there would undoubtedly be an increase, it would probably be minimal because the extent of the damages that the assured could recover for would in all cases be spelled out rather clearly in the insurance policy. The greatest obstacle to legislating no-fault insurance, according to the experiences of states that have wanted to try it, has been the opposition of trial lawyers. Such opposition is understandable since they would lose a large source of their business, but the welfare of trial lawyers is not the primary concern; the welfare of the citizenry is.

3. Divorce Litigation.

Another measure for limiting the costs of the judicial system is to strictly limit divorce litigation, another lucrative source of business for lawyers. At one time, it was very difficult to get a divorce in most states because there were not many grounds for it. Today, many states have the equivalent of no-fault divorce. That is, all the parties have to do is avoid living together for a year, and that is grounds enough. Limitations on litigated divorces, to the point of nearly eliminating them, are discussed in detail in Chapter 5. Divorce litigation also constitutes a large part of the civil caseload for courts, and a major reduction in the number of divorce cases would significantly reduce the costs to the people of the nation.

4. Legal Fees and Costs.

Yet another measure is to enact laws changing the current rule of long standing that the winners and losers each pay their own attorney fees and costs. The change would require that the loser and the loser's legal representative must pay the winner's fees and costs as well as their own. For example, if, by agreement under a contingency fee contract between the losing party and his attorney, the attorney was to receive one-third of the settlement or judgment, he would be required to pay one-third of the winner's fees and costs and receive no fee from the loser. The losing party would be required to pay the other two-thirds of the winner's fees and costs as well as his own costs. The number of frivolous lawsuits would be greatly curtailed.

5. Revocable Trusts.

One lucrative field for lawyers has been the probate of wills and the distribution of a deceased person assets according to his will or in accordance with the laws of intestate succession. The growing use of revocable trusts will gradually reduce the necessity for a lawyer at time of death.

6. Jury Trials.

Damages awarded by juries in civil cases are often unreasonably high. Juries themselves add significantly to the cost of trials and should be limited to felony cases. All other kinds of cases could be tried less expensively and, arguably, better by a single judge or, in some cases, by a panel of three-judges.

G. Repeal the Federal Income Tax Law and Substitute.

Nearly everyone agrees that the present income tax is a monstrosity and an abomination because of its complexities and because of the difficulties it poses for taxpayers in simply filling out the forms to pay their taxes.

Here's how Albert C. Crenshaw, a columnist writing for the Washington Post in April, 2001, described the federal income tax law and regulations:

Today's United States Tax Code contains 1,395,000 words – enough to fill 9,500 pages of very small print. There are another 8 million words of regulations – filling 20,000 pages – to help taxpayers figure out what the 1,395,000 words are saying. Then there are some 340 Internal Revenue Service publications, totaling more than 13,000 pages, to further clarify those 9,395,000 words of law and regulation. And finally, last year the IRS issued 58 new revenue rulings, 49 revenue procedures, 64 notices, 100 announcements and at least 2,400 private letter rulings and technical advice memoranda for taxpayers for whom the 9,395,000 words of law and regulation and the 13,000 pages of publications weren't enough. Even a fairly ordinary taxpayer filing a Form 1040 could be faced not only with the 79 lines on the form and 144 pages of instructions, but 11 schedules totaling 443 lines, including instructions; 19 separate worksheets within the instructions; plus 18 other "commonly used" forms.

The cost to the taxpayer in keeping records, trying to understand the instructions, and filling out the necessary forms takes a great deal of time and adds significantly to his costs over and above the amount he winds up paying to the Internal Revenue Service. Almost two-thirds of taxpayers fill out Form 1040, and the IRS estimates that they spend an average of just under 12 hours apiece doing it. Most hire a tax preparer. About half of those who file even the simple 1040EZ form hire a preparer.

The question is, <u>with what</u> does it need to be replaced? Two types of taxes have been extensively discussed and debated: a national sales tax and a flat tax.

1 . National Sales Tax.

This is a single-rate tax on consumer purchases of goods and services. The advantages of this tax are that the individual has no forms to fill out. He pays the tax when he makes a purchase, the same as he does now with the state or local sales taxes. A necessary bow to those with low incomes would be to exempt sales of food, prescription, and over-the-counter drugs. The amount of the tax that would have to be charged to provide the revenue necessary to support the federal government in its present size and form is variously estimated at between 15 and 23 percent The disadvantage of it is that some merchants may be tempted to sell their merchandise tax free or, after collecting the tax, not pay it to the government. Because the number of merchants filing would be far fewer than the number of individuals filing today, compliance enforcement would be much easier and cheaper.

2. Flat Tax.

This is a single-rate tax on all types of income advocated as a replacement for the present income tax. Corporations could be charged the same rate on all net income not paid out as dividends. Here again, the tax rate necessary to support the federal government is variously estimated at between 15 and 20 percent, with an exemption for low income families. The taxpayer would still have to file a return, but it would be a vastly less complicated form – probably a single page. A disadvantage is that, as it is today, politicians would be tempted to load it up with deductions, exemptions, and credits for their constituents or campaign contributors.

3. National Sales Tax and Flat Tax.

James K. Glassman, financial columnist, writing in the Washington Post, proposes a combination of the national sales tax and the flat tax with a tax rate of eight percent on each. The low rates would serve as a disincentive for merchants to cheat on collections of the sales tax and would deter politicians from loading up the flat tax.

4. Estate Tax (Escheat).

There is another tax that should be considered. We have seen that the wealth of a nation is determined for the most part by the size and quality of its work force. Excessive restrictions, regulations, taxes, or conditions of any kind on the freedom of workers, will prevent or inhibit them from becoming as productive as they can be and will result in national wealth which is less than optimal. Usually, it is a government that is excessively restrictive. It may be a monarchy, a theocracy, an oligarchy, a plutocracy or, less frequently, a democracy. Sometimes it can be the unavailability of suitable educational and health care systems for children which keeps them from growing up to be healthy, educated adults. But limitations on the access to capital that potential producers have will also result in production and wealth less than optimal.

The capitalist system is almost universally recognized as the best economic system in the world. Its big advantage over communism and socialism is that it allows the market to automatically set prices and control production through the natural operation of supply and demand. What is not commonly recognized is that capitalism, through embracing the right of inheritance, tends to foster the migration of wealth from the masses of potential producers into the hands of fewer and fewer individuals. Some diligent producers accumulate wealth during their working lives in excess of their needs. This wealth (capital) is available for investment and the production of yet more wealth. Their heirs may continue this process until a considerable fortune has been accumulated in a family over a generation or so. However, some of the heirs to such fortunes may have little motivation to extend themselves to be productive. Capital tied up in such fortunes restricts the availability of capital for others who may be more motivated and more productive if they had better access to capital.

We have a federal estate tax and state death taxes which tend to minimize the migration into the hands of a few of the wealthy under a capitalist system, but there are a number of legal devices, including foundations, that allow the wealthy to largely avoid these taxes and pass their wealth on to their heirs when they die. Laws need to be passed that would require foundations and similar estate tax avoidance instruments to be owned so that when the owners die, their property interest can be confiscated by the government and sold to others.

There was a practice during the Middle Ages known as escheat. When a lord died, his estate escheated to the Crown; that is, the Crown confiscated his property and sold it or traded it for military or other support. The federal estate tax also should also be confiscatory. As an exemption, spouses with children to raise should be able to retain it all until the youngest child reaches majority. At that time, the government would take one-half of what remained. unless the spouse had remarried, in which case the government would take all that remained. Spouses without children should be able to retain half of the deceased spouse's wealth until he or she dies, at which time the remainder would be confiscated. Guardians of children should have access to the entire fortune for purposes of raising the children until the youngest child reached adulthood. Then, the government would take all that was left.

The government would be required to sell the property that it confiscated at public auction within a short time after it was acquired. Such measures would not only free up capital for others, it would also help meet the financial needs of government and make for lower income and payroll taxes for workers (producers), assuming that the cost of government remained the same. Instead of concentrating on the accumulation of wealth, parents would be more inclined to give more personal attention to carefully raising and educating their children, thus enabling them to better cope with their lives and careers as adults. Owners of wealth during their lifetimes would also be more inclined to be more liberal in compensating employees and in donating money to churches and other charitable institutions if they knew it would all be lost when they died. Gifts, except to charities, would have to be heavily taxed and limited.

All of us at one time or another have sat down on a quiet Sunday afternoon to play the board game Monopoly. The banker doles out an equal amount of money to each player, and the game begins. If the game continues long enough, one player winds up with all of the properties and the money. That concludes the game. The next time the game is played, the players do not start where they left off in the last game. No. The banker once again doles out an equal amount of money to each player. Each generation in life is a new game, too, and the players need to start out on as equal a footing as possible. That is what a confiscatory estate tax would help to do.

Part II. The Producer/Eater Ratio

Section A. Optimizing the P/E Pipeline.

If there was a modern-day Paul Revere, his cry would be "The eaters are coming." Eaters are those adults in our society who consume – necessarily, of course – but do not produce as much as they consume, or produce nothing at all. Into this category would fall those adults of all ages who are too physically or mentally infirm to produce at least as much as they consume, those who have no marketable skills, those who are not sufficiently motivated to produce as much as they consume, those who have sufficient wealth that they do not have to – and do not – produce as much as they consume, and the prison population. Businesses, industries, and developing nations receiving government subsidies of any kind are also eaters. On the other hand, producers are adults who produce as many goods and services as they consume, or more. They are the common people. They produce the wealth of the nation. They include mothers, working in the home, caring for children and not supported by the public. They also include businesses and industries that do not receive government subsidies.

The reason for the cry is that the eaters are growing in absolute numbers as well as growing in relation to the number of producers in the United States. This situation places an ever-growing burden on the producers who provide support for the eaters. The ratio of producers to eaters is now estimated to be about four to one, which means that every four working adults are supporting one eater. In addition, every two working adults are supporting about 1.5 children. The situation is bad for producers now, but it will get worse. This is not a speculative prediction; it is inevitable. It is not that it *could* happen, or *might* happen. It *will* happen. We can easily see the problem by dividing the 262 million people in the United States five years of age and older into four age groups comprising approximately 20 years each. **Table 1** shows how they look:

Table 1.
Population of the United States
5 Years of Age and Older, Year 2000*

Age Group	No. of People (In Millions)
Under 5 years	19
Ages 5-24	80
Ages 25-44	85
Ages 45-64	62
Ages 65 and over	35

*Source: Bureau of the Census

As of the year 2000, the two age groups ages 25-64 years (147 million people – mostly producers – in the two groups combined) provide for the 35 million people – mostly eaters – in the age group 65 and over. This is a ratio of 4.2 to 1. When the group aged 45-65 (62 million persons) is fully retired in 20 years they will be provided for by the two age groups now ages 5 - 44 (totaling 165 million people). This is a ratio of 2.7 to 1, or a drastically reduced number of producers who will be supporting each retiree. Producers will also continue to have the nation's children to support, adding to their burden.

Considering the number of eaters in the age group 25-64 (about 9 million), the ratio of producers to eaters is now slightly less than 4 to 1 at this time, and will be close to 2 to 1 in 20 years. As the large population bulge of baby boomers retire, some of them (like current retirees) will become funded eaters. A funded eater is one who has accumulated enough assets that he can pay producers to provide for him. Unfunded eaters have no assets or insufficient assets, and rely on producers paid by government or charitable institutions to provide for them.

There are several indications that the ratio of producers to consumers has become too small already. One, of course, is high taxes. Another is the nation's chronic annual budget deficit, the related growth in the national debt, and (naturally) the growth in the cost of servicing the debt. Budget deficits are the result of government spending more than its citizens are willing to pay. Even with high taxes, the nation's infrastructure is deteriorating as more and more of the nation's annual finite production of wealth is siphoned off to provide for the eaters. Then there is the enormous and burdensome body of law and regulations to consider that has been built up over the years, much of which is to provide for the eaters.

There is a relationship between the number of eaters and the size and, naturally, the cost of government. As the number of eaters grows, so does government. Conversely, the rapidly growing population of eaters in the United States is attributable in large measure to programs of the federal government (such as the Supplemental Security Income program) which make it possible to exist as an eater. Welfare is another such program (although it is not as fulfilling for individuals to go on welfare today as it was before the welfare reform program). The same is true for manufacturing, agricultural and service companies, and other nations that are enjoying government subsidies of one kind or another. The federal government has created a dependency on the part of the eaters to the extent that many would not be able to survive for long if the program(s) benefitting them were withdrawn. Therefore, some of these programs, if terminated suddenly, would cause great hardship and should, if possible, be phased out over a period of time to allow recipient individuals, companies, industries and other nations a chance to adjust.

There is no mystery about how to maximize the number of producers and to minimize the number of eaters. There are only four basic ways to do it. The way most acceptable to society for improving the producer/eater ratio is to enhance the family environment in which children and young men and women are reared, and upgrade the schools in which they are educated. It is well documented that, where the mother in a two-parent family stays home and rears the children, they are much more likely to grow up to be producers. Governments are and have been trying to improve schools, but governments allow easy marriages and, for all parents including those with children, easy divorces which are counterproductive in providing home environments optimal for children. Childhood is the pipeline to adulthood, and the objective is to increase the number of producers emerging from the pipeline and minimize the number of eaters. While this is the best of the four ways in terms of acceptability to society, its full effect will not be felt for years.

The second way is to reduce the number of potential eaters entering the pipeline; that is, being born. These would be unwanted children children that no married couple is able and willing to raise and children who have serious birth conditions or defects that are not correctable at all or are correctable only at great expense. Such children, if allowed to enter the pipeline, will have to be raised by society, and those with serious birth defects will require extraordinary care from society as children and likely, for all of their natural lives. At present, government efforts in this regard are restricted to discouraging out-of-wedlock pregnancies by promoting celibacy and the use of condoms. These measures contribute only to reducing the number of newborns, but are not specific as to reducing the number of them likely to be eaters.

The third way to improve the producer/eater ratio is to reduce the size of existing eater pools by reducing the inflow of unproductive immigrants into the country and the number of those already in the country, by reducing the size of the prison population, and by reducing the number of subsidies from the governmental to individuals, domestic companies, industries and foreign countries. The third way has an immediate beneficial effect on the producer/eater ratio, but the government does little or nothing to reduce eater pools.

The fourth way, which also produces immediate results, is by terminating existing lives. These would include unwanted embryos or fetuses (abortions), newborns with serious defects and those who are unwanted by either biological or adoptive parents able and willing to raise them (birthed feticide),aged and infirm individuals who wish to die (assisted suicide), and old people afflicted with Alzheimer's or who are otherwise deprived of their cognitive capabilities and who have no responsibility in society (eutheanasia). Some people may regard this way as unduly cruel, callous and, therefore, unacceptable, but everything must be considered relatively. The alternative may well be future inter-generational conflict.

Chapter 5. Enhancing Environments for Children.

A. Early Marriages.

Probably, the best time for a woman to have children is in her late teens or early twenties. It is then that she is flexible and adaptable, she has the energy and endurance to be up to the task, she is most fertile, and is least likely to bear children with birth defects. According to an article published in <u>USA Today</u> in July 2002, a Rutgers University study released in June, 2002, citing a government-funded survey of high school students from 1996-2000, found that 38 percent of senior-class men and 29 percent of senior-class women believe that marriage leads to a fuller and happier life. Another 1994 government-funded survey cited by the article found that 59 percent of unmarried men and 48 percent of unmarried women ages 18-35 wanted to get married. With these kinds of beliefs and desires, why do men now wait until the median age of 27 years of age and women 25 years to get married? There must be dozens of reasons, but I submit that the main one is the disparity between the income they would have as young newlyweds and the standard of living they have each come to expect as working singles, especially if they were living at home with their parents for free.

Throughout early American history, life was a lot simpler than it is most everywhere in the United States today. Let's take colonial America. A few years after young people achieved puberty in colonial days, they were just about equivalent to any adult when it came to making a living. Very little education was needed. Most of what one needed to know was learned from one's parents. The country had an agrarian economy, and people made their living mostly by working small farms. To start a farm, a young couple had to acquire a piece of land. Sometimes their parents could give them a piece of their land or they might have rented it. Sometimes they may have had to work as hired hands on someone else's land for a few years to save enough money to rent or buy a piece of land of their own. The land would usually have been wooded. They had to cut down the trees, some of which they – with the help of family, friends, and neighbors – used to build a cabin. Others they split and used to make fences. The rest were burned. The soil between the stumps was tilled and planted. Food that they produced by farming was supplemented by hunting, fishing, and trapping. At this point, the young couple was on a par with their parents and their neighbors. They were producers. They were, perhaps, 15 or 16 years of age. If they were not married, they were financially able to get married and begin having children. Material standards were low. Within a few years after puberty, they were able to satisfy their sexual appetites in a way approved by society.

Reflect on the difference between then and today. Today we have in the United States a complex, technical economy and a materialistic society. In most jurisdictions, young people must, by law, attend public school until they are 16 years of age. The average student does not graduate and receive a diploma until he is 18 years of age. Those who drop out of school before receiving a diploma have reduced employment prospects for the rest of their lives. The high school diploma is enough for some jobs, but many jobs require a college degree. This means another four years in school at considerable expense to the student and his parents before he is ready to offer himself for employment. By this time, the student is 22 years old, and may be rather deep in debt. More years may pass before he is financially able to set up a household and provide for a family.

Young couples need to lower their sights with respect to their hoped-for life-style and material standard of living to bring them down to the level of income they can reasonably expect the husband to be able to earn at first. They need to save before they marry and otherwise conserve their resources. Instead of an expensive diamond ring as an engagement gift, they agree on a zircon. Instead of a large church wedding and reception, they settle for an elopement or a civil ceremony before a justice of the peace with only a few close friends and relatives present. They take a short wedding trip or none at all. After they are married, they forgo trying to afford a nice house or apartment, such as the ones they may have been living in with their parents. At the very bottom, they think in terms of renting a furnished room at first and graduating upward in housing accommodations as their income increases. Instead of occasional weekend skiing trips to Vail and spring breaks in Florida, they take pleasure in movies at the local cinema. They may have to substitute evenings at home playing Monopoly or Scrabble for wild concerts or all-night parties out on the town. Thus, couples willing to make the necessary adjustments in their lifestyle can avoid debt and live on the husband's income (small though it may be), save at least the wife's income, get married early, have children and lead happy lives. However, they should not think of having children until the husband's income will at the least allow them to rent a small house or apartment and at least partially furnish it. This is financial planning. Parents also need to help the young couple financially to the extent that they can.

Then, when they have children, the wife can stay home and take care of them during their tender years, and they can live on the husband's income. It is an excellent arrangement. The practice surely benefits the children who have their mother at home all the time to care for them. The couple benefits because they do not have to lead the frenetic lives that many couples lead today when both work outside the home. Schools benefit because parents have the time and energy to cooperate with school authorities and to encourage their children to behave in school and to try their best to learn. Society as a whole benefits because parents provide for their own children without burdening society. It doesn't take a village to raise a child; it takes two devoted parents.

B. Mothers Stay Home.

The bearing and rearing of children is by far the most important function of any society. This is where society's future producers originate. Women are natural to the function by virtue of being born with reproductive organs, milk-producing glands on their chests for feeding infants and (usually) gentle dispositions. Bearing and rearing children is uniquely a woman's role. The great disservice done by women's rights organizations was to demean the role of mothers and homemakers. Raising children is indeed a difficult, time-consuming and sometimes exasperating task, but there are rewards that cannot be realized in any other way. Here is the way Tracy Thompson, a journalist with the <u>Washington Post</u> who elected to quit her job and stay home with her newborn daughter Emma, described some of her experiences in a <u>Post</u> article:

> *Emma made it past the newborn stage and became a settled baby, and, like countless mothers before me, I discovered this new job could be fun. I spent a lot of time every day lying on the floor next to her, making nonsense sounds, watching her discover her toes. I'd put my face up to hers, and she would try to bite my nose, making little baby pants the whole time – <u>Hah</u> . . . . <u>hah</u>! – and squeals of delight. Some mornings, I would steal into her room and find her quietly awake, amusing herself. When she saw me, her whole body would go rigid with anticipation*

– mouth a perfect O, arms and legs outstretched, waving;
Pick me up! Come play!

Mothers need to be educated. When one considers that children spend more time and learn more at home than they ever do in school, and that the mother is the principal teacher at home, it is apparent that – although she doesn't need to be a rocket scientist – it is useful for her to know about a wide range of subjects. Women also need to know how to nurture and care for children and babies in particular. When a baby arrives on the scene, most mothers are at a loss for knowing how to care for it. What they know about mothering they learned by watching their own mothers. If their mother was a good mother, they will likely be a good mother too. If not, neither is she likely to be a good mother. For this reason, mothering needs to be a required course for female students in all high schools. The course, at a minimum, should teach nutrition, substances and practices to avoid while pregnant, handling of babies, what to expect as they develop, common ailments of babies and young children, what to do about such ailments, the importance of medical and dental checkups, the importance of extended breast feeding, and the importance of play, touching, fondling, holding, hugging, reading, music, and talking.

We have to begin with the proposition that the likelihood of a child growing up to become a producer instead of an eater is greatly enhanced if the child is born or adopted into a family with parents who stay married and where the mother can stay home, breast feed the infants, rear the children herself, and not put them out to day care. This proposition is well grounded.

A study conducted by the National Institute of Child Health and Human Development of 1,364 children for the first seven years of their lives indicated that children in day care are inclined to be more aggressive than other children. Other studies have found that children growing up in single-parent homes –

where they are usually put out to day care – are four times more likely to grow up to engage in criminal behavior and three times more likely to become welfare recipients; i.e., become eaters.

The results of another government-sponsored study, the largest and most authoritative of child care and development of its kind ever conducted, which tracked 1,300 children at ten sites across the country since 1991, were presented at a meeting of the Society for Research in Child Development in Minneapolis in 2001. The study revealed that 17 percent of children who spent over 30 hours a week in child care demonstrated problem behaviors by the time they were between the ages of 4 ½ and 6. Only 6 percent of those who spent less than 10 hours a week in such care had the same problems. These behavioral problems included aggressiveness, disobedience and defiancé. However, it was found that high quality child care improved children's language and memory skills.

The University of Washington conducted a study of early child care which was funded by the National Institute of Child Health and Human Development. Most of the infants in the study started regular day care for at least 10 hours weekly by four months of age. The study found that half of all infants under age one were being routinely cared for by someone other than their mother, and that fewer than one in ten children ages three and under are likely to receive excellent care.

There are other equally compelling studies that support the proposition that babies breast-fed for at least the first six months of their lives will be healthier, happier, more intelligent and, therefore, grow up more likely to become producers. The American Academy of Pediatrics urges mothers to breast-feed for a year, with a minimum of six months. About two-thirds of mothers nurse their infants during the first week of life, but less than one-third are still breast-feeding after six months and only 15 percent after a year. Regardless of their mother's IQ, education, and other socioeconomic factors, two studies found that breast-fed babies scored significantly higher on IQ tests when they grew up.

Also, a Harvard University study found that the longer infants are breast-fed, the less likely they are to become overweight by the time they reach their teenage years. Besides scoring significantly higher on IQ tests when grown and being less inclined to overweight, numerous studies have found that breast-fed babies are less likely than formula-fed babies to suffer from diarrhea and intestinal infections, are less inclined to develop pulmonary and urinary tract infections, and have significantly fewer earaches, colds, eczema, asthma, and other allergies. A study published recently in the American Journal of Clinical Nutrition found that babies given cow's-milk-based formula instead of breast milk have higher blood pressure as adults.

A recent Scandinavian study that analyzed feeding information from parents of 244 babies who died of sudden infant death syndrome compared to similar information from parents of 869 healthy babies, found that babies who were breast-fed for less than eight weeks were between three and five times more likely to die from SIDS than babies breast-fed for four or more months. The study did not speculate on why this was so.

The composition of breast milk – of which a healthy baby can consume up to 30 ounces a day, depending on the baby's size – actually changes from time to time according to the needs of the infant – another miracle associated with birth. The lower incidence of disease among breast-fed babies has not only to do with the healthful quality of breast milk over formula, but is also probably due in some measure to mothers who, to breast-feed, almost have to be at home (along with their babies, of course) where the babies are not exposed to the sicknesses of other children. As beneficial as breast-feeding over formula feeding appears to be, the federal government encourages formula-feeding through the Women, Infants and Children program which purchases for poor women about half of all the infant formula sold in the United States. It is white women and wealthy women who tend to breast-feed the most.

There are benefits to mothers from breast-feeding as well, apart from the sensual pleasure of it. A study done by the Collaborative Group on Hormonal Factors in Breast Cancer, a British research group led by an Oxford University epidemiologist and published in the *Lancet,* concluded in 2002 that a woman's relative risk of breast cancer declines by 7 percent with each birth and by an additional 4.5 percent with each year that she breast-feeds. Doctors at Brigham & Women's Hospital in Boston say that breast-feeding may help mothers avoid rheumatoid arthritis.

A mother does not have to have studies to know that she needs to stay home with her young children. All she needs to do is to obey her maternal instincts, which cry out for her to stay with her children of tender ages and nurture them. If she obeys these instincts, she will be happy; if she does not, she will feel years of anguish and guilt. Having children does not mean simply dropping the offspring onto the bed sheet in the delivery room. That is just the beginning. It takes years of hard work, personal care, and attention to raise children. It is not natural to abandon them to somebody else after they are born. Beasts in the wild do better than that as parents. One – usually the female – or both parents of nearly all animals other than humans look after their own young. Women, please, either stay home to raise and breast-feed your young children or take a pass and don't have them at all. If you can't rear them, don't bear them.

Nevertheless, according to Labor Department figures, two-thirds of mothers with preschool children worked away from home at least part-time in 1997. They did this although a study by the Manhattan-based nonprofit policy group, Public Agenda, found that 70 percent of parents with children of 5 years of age and younger believed that one parent staying home was the best arrangement during a child's early years. Such a belief was justified according to the study of 230 day care centers by the Child Care Workforce which found that most child care was barely adequate because of high turnover of personnel, low wages, and lack of on-site training. In light of these sobering facts, why do mothers place their babies in someone else's hands to care for them during the day?

Some children are placed in someone else's care when they are only a few weeks or months old. Sometimes, it is a day care center. Sometimes, it is an au pair, sometimes a neighbor, or someone just making a few dollars on the side. In some cases, the care giver is a relative. Even with a relative, children do not receive the same care, encouragement, and nurturing as they would from a loving mother. Sometimes, when they are older and in school, there is nobody at all to look out for them after school. These, so-called latchkey children are particularly prone to trouble after school when no parent is home.

Many of society's problems with children today can be traced to the fact that mothers do not stay home with their preschool children, and that at least one parent is not at home when their older children leave for school in the morning and when they come home after school in the afternoon. Included are problems with drugs, alcohol, tobacco, juvenile crime, gangs, and discipline problems (both at home and in school) that, in turn, adversely affect their children's education. When the two working parents are home, they are often hard-pressed to find time to spend with their children. They are too exhausted to help them with their homework and to motivate them to learn. The federal Study of Adolescent Health mentioned below found that the mere presence of parents at home in the morning, after school, at dinner, and at bedtime made it less likely that teenagers would use alcohol, tobacco, and marijuana. The government's answers to this problem are more stringent standards for day care, bigger tax deductions for parents with children in day care, and more and bigger subsidies for day care centers themselves.

Children born out of wedlock and children of broken homes are in a worse situation than children of a family with both parents working. Most of them live with single mothers working outside the home as the sole provider, or on welfare. Their mothers often don't want them to begin with and are ill-prepared to support them. Some are badly abused and even killed by a parent, stepparent, or live-in companion of the mother. When they reach school age, they often do not receive the support they need in the way of daily encouragement, a proper home study environment, decent clothes, spending money for little things like fees to go on field trips, class rings and the like – things that mean a lot to students and are necessary for them to hold their own socially and excel academically. When there is no father living with the family, children – and particularly, male children – suffer from lack of a role model and a stabilizing influence in their lives.

Worse yet, they may wind up in a foster home (and frequently more than one) until they reach the age of 18 and are then dumped out on the street to shift for themselves. It is estimated that there are now more than 500,000 children in foster care in the United States. By reason of changes in address of the welfare mother's residence dictated by the local welfare department or by reason of reassignments of children in foster homes from one to another, children are often assigned to one school, then another and yet another. Budding relationships with teachers and friendships with other students are lost, and these children have to start all over again each time. A $25 million federal study, known as the National Longitudinal Study of Adolescent Health, and published in the Journal of the American Medical Association in 1997, found that teenagers who have strong emotional attachments to parents and teachers are less likely to use drugs and alcohol, attempt suicide, engage in violence, or become sexually active at an early age.

In two-parent families, matters need to be arranged so that mothers can stay at home full time with children of pre-kindergarten ages and to be at home when their older children leave for school in the morning and when they come home from school in the afternoon. Why is that important? First, children who stay at home with their mothers during the formative years tend to be healthier, and especially so if they are breast fed. Mothers at home are in a better position to detect illness early on and have it treated. In a day care center, the sickness of one child frequently spreads rapidly to the other children – and, thence, to the parents at home. Second, children get the attention they need from stay-at-home mothers, attention that day care providers cannot give them. In the early years, children are more secure with their mothers present, and they grow up to be more confident and self-assured. When they go to school, they are willing to take on tasks that they might not otherwise have the confidence to try. They learn better. More than anything else, children want the approval of their parents – especially their mothers – and they will extend themselves in all of their endeavors trying to get it. It is thus that good students and good producers develop.

A parent at home when the children are at home helps children to stay out of trouble. Recently, two male students appeared in a Fairfax County, Virginia, high school wearing short dresses and black fishnet stockings. Can you imagine these boys walking out the door of their home dressed like that for school under the watchful gaze of their father or mother? Their parents had to have had already left for work when these young fellows left for school. When children come home from school and their mother is there with a snack of milk and cookies and ready to talk, she is going to notice if they have been using drugs. She will learn about problems they are having at school or possible gang activity. She will be in a much better position to cooperate with the children's teachers and school authorities.

A popular notion of why mothers choose to work outside the home is that they do it to offset the diminished earnings of their husbands. That is, mothers have to work outside the home so the family can eat. No doubt some mothers are in this situation, but Robert J. Samuelson, writing for the <u>Washington Post,</u> says that the facts do not generally support this notion. Women first entered the workforce in numbers in the 1950s and 1960s when men's wages were rising. The growth in men's wages has slowed since the early 1970s, but the increase in the number of wives with jobs since the early 1970's is concentrated among upper income couples who need the extra money the least.

The year 2000 median per capita income for men under 65 years of age in the United States was a little over $30,000, which should be more than enough to put a roof overhead, food on the table, and provide clothes for a family. It is enough, of course, but some of those starting out on their careers do not make this much. The problems are simply that the material standards men are required to meet are too high and that governments (federal, state, and local taken together) do not allow them to keep enough of what they make. Some scholars estimate that governments now take as much as 35 percent of the average wage earner's income when all kinds of taxes and fees of all governments (federal, state and local) are considered.

There are other more plausible reasons for parents putting their children out to day care. Single and divorced mothers with no other support have no choice. Similarly, married couples who have maneuvered themselves into a financial strait jacket have no real choice. How tragic, because this option almost always results in a long-term psychological and social disadvantage for the children, but is to the immediate economic advantage of the parents – as they see it. Although, at times, the income a mother can make at a job outside the home is only marginally in excess of the additional costs associated with her working outside the home, parents still do it. In some of these cases, working outside the home would not be cost-efficient at all were it not for tax credits and other governmental subsidies for day care. Governments, in this way, subsidize a practice detrimental to young children. Why would politicians enact legislation detrimental to children? The answer is easy. Children do not vote; parents do. Children would be benefitted if the government subsidized stay-at-home mothers instead of day care centers.

Another plausible reason children are put out to day care is that the mother has been told by women's organizations that she can have career and children concurrently and is not aware that by doing so she will create problems for her children in the long run. Sadly, there may be other mothers who are fully aware of the downside of day care and may not be in financial straits at all but are simply willing to sacrifice their babies and young children on the altar of their own careers.

C. Having It All.

Women's rights organizations have trumpeted the message that women can have it all, both careers *and* children. This, too, women can do, but doing it requires careful planning if the children are not to be compromised. She can have both without compromising the children but only consecutively – not concurrently. Children first and then the career. How can a woman arrange to be at home full time with her preschool children? She needs to marry a man who has money and income, and is willing to support her and their children by himself – or who has good prospects for being able to do so. A wag once opined that a successful man is one who makes more money than his wife can spend; a successful woman is one who finds a man like that.

This is what women wanting to have children should strive for. This is the most important factor. Arranged marriages in some other countries emphasize this factor. Another factor – but one of far less importance for women – is sexual attraction. This is important because she is going to have to sleep for a long time with the man she chooses as a husband. It is helpful if this does not become a burdensome duty. For young men, on the other hand, it is most important to marry a woman with a sexual appetite to match their own. Other factors like good looks, pleasant demeanor, outstanding physique, good health, a positive attitude, and a witty mind are all important to both sexes, but all are subordinate to the first two.

A woman who has her eye on a man willing to marry her but without sufficient savings or income has choices. The best one, probably, is to proceed with marriage but for the couple to lower their living standards so that, even after children come, they can live on the husband's income. Or she may simply decide to live with him childless until he is in a position to support her and their children by himself, and then marry. There doesn't appear to be any social stigma about this arrangement anymore. Young and old alike are doing it. According to a Census Bureau survey, more than 4 million American couples live together without being married. Unmarried senior citizens are cohabiting in record numbers. More than 30 percent of women aged 19 to 24 are currently living with a partner, says the Director of the University of Southern California Marriage and Family Program.

Or they might live separately, both work and save their money until they reached a point that his income, together with their accumulated savings, would be enough to support the family during the early years in the lifestyle they choose, and then marry. Or she might begin her career, marry, interrupt her career when children are born, and then continue with her career after they are raised to school age. In any of these cases, she should delay beginning or continuing her career until after all of the children reached school age. Feminists will complain that this puts women years behind men of the same age in their careers. They should not complain. Women have a life expectancy about five years longer than men on the average and should expect to work to an older age than men before retirement, so it tends to even out. In all of these cases, couples need to adjust their living standards to be commensurate with what the husband can provide by himself.

Once a woman's children are all raised to school age and she wishes to work outside the home, she will usually need a work schedule of less than eight hours a day that will permit her to be home when the children go to school in the morning and when they come home in the afternoon. Women who are self-employed can often make suitable scheduling arrangements. Currently, some full-time jobs in the public schools work out this way, as do some sales jobs and some clerical jobs. Part-time jobs are sometimes easily scheduled to suit. When possible, employers need more and more to arrange job schedules so that women with school age children can work part-time. Later on, when the children all out of school, it would be helpful if such mothers were able to switch to the regular eight-hour day, if desired. It may well be to the employer's benefit to do this at any time to help insure continuity of experienced employees, but it is particularly of an advantage to employers in times of labor shortages.

These days, women are able to work outside the home after all of their children are raised to school age without compromising responsibilities at home because of the many labor saving devices that now exist – if the family can afford them. Seventy years ago, women had to iron all of the cotton clothes, sheets and pillowcases. Today, fabrics blended of cotton and polyester need no ironing except, possibly, for touching up collars and cuffs. Then, women had to hang the carpets out on the clothesline and manually beat the dust out of them with a wire beater. Today electric vacuum sweepers do a much better job quicker and easier. In those days, houses in many areas were heated with bituminous coal. In the winter, soot was everywhere. A thorough, top-to-bottom housecleaning was required every spring. Today, most residences are heated with natural gas or oil with far less dirt. Then, women washed clothes on a corrugated zinc and wooden scrubbing board, rinsed them, wrung them by hand, put up clotheslines and hung them outside to dry. Today, the automatic clothes washer and dryer have made easy work of washing clothes. The microwave oven and electric dishwasher are other examples. Then, all foods had to be prepared from scratch. Today there are lots of prepared and semi-prepared foods on the grocer's shelves that require little more than heating. The list goes on.

Women who do not have children and do not want to have any should be able to enter the workplace outside the home on *about* the same footing as men. One advantage this country has over many other countries is that women are allowed more freely to utilize their God-given talents and abilities in the workplace outside the home. There are laws, regulations, and court decisions on the books in the United States to insure that women are treated the same as men. However, married men with children should have preference in the workplace because they have legally enforceable obligations for supporting families. Veterans (usually men) should also have preference because of having fulfilled a legally enforceable obligation for defending the country. Men between the ages of 18 and 26 are required to register for the draft on pain of a possible $250,000 fine and a five-year prison term. Having registered, they may be called up in a draft to perform duty hazardous to life and limb in defense of the country. These are obligations that women generally do not have. These men deserve some preference.

If women choose to enter the workplace outside the home and take a pass on having children, they should resign themselves to an inevitable long-time aching void in their childless lives. Germain Greer was once a leader in the twentieth century feminist movement. As reported by Charles Krauthammer in one of his Washington Post columns, she wrote in the British magazine *Aura* about the terrible sorrow she feels about her lost chance for motherhood. She tells of the time she cared for the infant daughter of a friend saying that the infant lit up her life in a way that nobody, certainly no lover, had ever done. She said that she was not prepared for the sensuousness of the infant and her innocent love.

D. The Marriage Contract.

I submit that men and women marry for different reasons. Men marry for sex, companionship and children in that order; women marry for children, companionship, and sex in that order. Men are motivated primarily by their appetite for sex, and women are motivated primarily by their nesting instinct.

Couples marrying actually enter into two contracts: one with each other and the second with the state. The actual contracts are never mentioned in the wedding ceremony. The bride and groom exchange vows before a clergyman or another official authorized to perform marriages, usually with an audience of friends and relatives in attendance, and usually with a great deal of pomp. The marriage vows contain many lovely words such as "to love and to cherish in sickness and health'til death do us part" et cetera. The ceremony is concluded with a ring on the finger of the bride and sometimes rings for both the bride and groom. The purpose of the ceremony is to fix in the minds of the newlyweds and those in attendance at the ceremony the obligations to one another that each of them has undertaken. Although so intended, this is not what one would call a binding contract as evidenced by the high divorce rate in this country.

A bride's actual contractual obligation to her groom is to both bear and rear children and provide natural (penis/vaginal) sex for her husband on a regular basis in return for protection and support. None of her obligations are legally enforceable. How could a court possibly enforce them? Women who have been accustomed to granting or denying sexual favors at their whim and fancy before marriage often fail to recognize that they have entered into a contract to provide regular vaginal sex for their husbands. At first, providing regular natural sex may be a joy and a pleasure for the wife, but after children come, it may become something more of a chore and a duty.

The husband's remedies when the wife unreasonably withholds sex are not anything nearly as good as those that the wife has if he fails in his obligations. In fact, he has no legal remedy at all. Most commonly, husbands simply put up with denied sex; that is, they sit in the doghouse. At other times, they may knock the wife about a bit in hopes of causing her to be more acquiescent (now an enforced criminal offense), or they may enter into an adulterous relationship with another woman (perhaps, grounds for divorce). Finally, he may walk away and desert the family. If the couple has children, this course is most reprehensible.

The husband's obligations under the contract are to protect and provide support for his wife and their children (at least until the youngest child reaches adulthood) in return for regular sex and children. That is quite a contract, and, unlike a wife's obligations, a husband's obligation for support, at least, is legally enforceable by the courts. What else can the courts do? If a man cannot be legally bound to provide for his wife and children, society has to do it, but society doesn't want to do it. Women are often heard to despair that men are reluctant to "make a commitment." Is it any wonder? The contract for the husband is more burdensome today than it ever was before because children today – both male and female – want to go to college when they come of age, which is a huge expense.

In most states, a divorced husband named by the wife as the father of a child is legally required to support it, even though he is not the father. This is because, in the absence of any way to determine paternity for sure, the husband is presumed to be the father. This presumption is made because, if the husband is not legally required to support the child, the state will have to. But, the state does not want to do that. Today, DNA testing makes the presumption unnecessary. Husbands and former husbands should have – and should have to be informed of – their legal right to have the baby DNA tested at birth, so that there is no lingering question as to paternity.

Two people living together can probably do so as cheaply or cheaper than they could living separately. However, when children are born into the family, it's a different story. And it's not just baby-related expenses; children are very expensive all of their lives. According to a U.S. Department of Agriculture consumer expenditure survey of 5,000 households, the average family with a child born in 2000 can expect to spend $166,000 for food, shelter and other basic necessities over the next 17 years. Adjusted for inflation, the total is $234,000. Four years of college is more yet, ranging on average from a cost of about $8,000 a year at state institutions for room, board and tuition (for in-state students) to about $20,000 for private institutions. These costs may be higher now, at about $9,000 and $25,000, respectively.

Men are also legally required to provide protection for the family. It is a natural responsibility because men are usually bigger and stronger than their wives and children and are less averse to confronting danger. Most of the protection for the home and family is provided by the police these days and is paid for with the taxes families pay. In most states, husbands and fathers do have some legal latitude for defending their families and would probably be considered remiss if they did not. Whether married or not, the Selective Service Act of the United States, signed into law in 1940, requires that young men reaching the age of 18 years register for Selective Service (the draft). When the government thinks the occasion demands it, registrants can be and are called up and pressed into service to defend the country. These are the same young men whom society asks to postpone natural sex for 13 or 14 years after puberty. Women are not required to register for the draft. They have no duty to protect the country. How could they have and still have the principal responsibility for raising children?

E. The Marriage License.

There is a second contract which is between the couple and the state. Before pledging their troth at the altar, they have to get a marriage license issued by the state, which license is evidence of the second contract. The marriage license needs to be recognized for what it really is; namely, a contract between the couple and the state for the benefit of the couple's children − not for the benefit of the couple − to better ensure that the couple stays together and raises their children. Appropriately, it should be renamed as a License to Have Children.

In most jurisdictions today, it is easier to get a marriage license than it is to get a driver's license. To get a driver's license, a person usually has to be 16 to 18 years of age, pay a fee, and pass a vision test, a written test, and a practical driving test. A man and a woman, each of whom usually has to be 18 years of age (younger sometimes with the consent of parents), can get a marriage license by simply paying to local government a nominal fee, getting a blood test (in most states) to detect the presence of sexually transmitted disease, and then sometimes sitting out a waiting period ranging from zero up to 60 days. This needs to change.

They should have to complete a questionnaire inquiring into their finances so that society can have some assurance that they have enough money to set up a household and that the husband has some means of producing income adequate to maintain the family. The questionnaire should include such questions as where the husband works, how long he has been employed there, how much income he earns, the name of the couple's bank, what kind of outstanding debts they have that might make it impossible for them to support a family (mortgages, car payments, credit card balances et cetera). Before issuing the license, the local government should check all answers with the couple's employers and creditors to make sure they are truthful. Standards would have to be set and met. Information would also need to be requested regarding previous marriages of either party and whether there were minor children of the marriage(s) still living. The existence of such children would normally preclude issuance of a license.

Equally important would be questions about alcohol, drug, and nicotine (smoking) habits which they (particularly the wife) may have that would be detrimental to the health of their offspring. A study by researchers at the federal Center for Disease Control and Prevention in Atlanta and published in the *Journal of Obstetrics and Gynecology* in August 1998 concluded that 12.8 percent of pregnant women in the U.S. used alcohol. Drinking by pregnant women can lead to a devastating array of irreversible physical, neurological and behavioral problems in children. Alcohol is the leading known preventable cause of mental retardation. Couples applying for a marriage license should be required to show that they had taken a suitable course including information about the devastating effect on the fetus of smoking, drinking alcoholic beverages, and taking various kinds of drugs, prescribed and over-the-counter as well as illegal.

Ann Streissguth, director of the Fetal Alcohol Syndrome and Drug Unit at the University of Washington Medical Center, says that babies born with fetal alcohol syndrome suffer from a variety of physical and mental defects including abnormally-formed organs, small brains, poor coordination, short attention spans and mental retardation. Many of the symptoms do not appear until the child is older. There is no way to test a baby for alcohol exposure, although their facial features may be a tip-off to a trained observer in extreme cases. Alcohol causes more damage to the fetus than illegal drugs. According to a study published in the *Journal of the American Medical Association* in April 2002, a fetus exposed to cocaine is twice as likely by age two to suffer from delayed mental development as a fetus not so exposed.

The findings of a study, conducted by researchers from the University of Chicago Medical Center and the University of Pittsburgh and published in the July 1997 issue of the *Archives of General Psychiatry*, not only confirmed a link between smoking among pregnant women and abnormal brain development of fetuses apparently caused by nicotine, but also concluded that sons of women who smoked over half a pack of cigarettes a day are four times more likely than sons of women who did not smoke to grow up displaying such antisocial behavior as lying, setting fires, vandalism, physical cruelty, forcible sexual activity, and stealing. A study conducted by researchers at the University of Pittsburgh showed that babies of mothers who had just one drink of an alcoholic beverage a day while pregnant had stunted growth decades later.

Although society does not care anymore if a couple simply cohabits without the benefit of marriage, what society does care about is that, if the couple has children, they be in a financial position to afford them and that the couple be free of diseases and conditions that would adversely affect any children they might have. Although an old U.S. Supreme Court decision has held that parenthood is an inherent constitutional right, no such right is actually mentioned in the U.S. Constitution, and society needs to recognize that having children is not a right, but only a privilege for those who have the capability and the willingness to raise healthy children.

Periodically, a clamor is raised by those on minimum wage (and their supporters inside and outside the Congress) that the minimum wage is not enough on which to raise a family. People on minimum wage are being subsidized by the state and should not be allowed the privilege of a family. Only when they have improved their financial position to a certain level should they be allowed to start a family. It does not take much money for a single adult to lead a satisfying and even rewarding life. Such people on low incomes are prime candidates for living in boarding houses or living at home with their parents and paying room and board. It is when a couple has children that costs escalate.

If one accepts the proposition that children born out of wedlock do not have nearly as good of a chance to become productive adults as do those born in wedlock (who are more likely to be cared for and breast fed by the mother during their tender years), then it would seem to be in the interest of society to both minimize the number of births out of wedlock and to make arrangements for those offspring that are born out of wedlock to be immediately adopted by a married couple willing and able to care for and support them, instead of being left with the single mother or placed in a foster home. Governments are currently subsidizing both single mothers and foster parents.

What happens if an unmarried mother gives birth in a hospital? It would be the same answer for a married couple on welfare or who had been on welfare as late as three months before the date of birth. If the unmarried parents would not marry or could not qualify for a license to marry, the next thing would be to arrange for the immediate adoption of the infant. Adoption agencies would have to keep lists at hospitals of pre-approved straight, married couples of good moral character ready, willing, and financially able to adopt a newborn so that the adoption could take place immediately after its birth. As soon as the child was born (assuming it did not have a serious defect, abnormality, condition or disease not correctable or correctable only at great expense), a couple on the list would immediately adopt the child, and it would be theirs without any legal claim by the natural parents. According to research done by psychologist L. Dianne Borders of the University of North Carolina at Greensboro, adopted kids are every bit as well-adjusted, socially skilled and intellectually able as their peers raised by natural parents. The timing of the adoption (the earlier in a child's life, the better) and the quality of parenting afterward are the factors that determine how adopted children thrive.

Further, legislation is needed requiring unmarried women who become pregnant and do not marry before the birth to forfeit their legal right to the child in favor of the state to put up for adoption. Thus, only married couples would be allowed to have children because they have entered into a long-term contract and have been licensed. The license should include a covenant between the state and the couple that they agree to stay together and care for and support their children until all of them are of age as adults. The contract should require further that the couple agrees to order their affairs so that the wife, as the mother of any children that issue from the union, can stay home full time to care for the children until the youngest reaches school age, and so that the mother can be home when the older children leave in the morning for school and when they return in the afternoon.

What would happen if there was not available a pre-approved couple willing and able to adopt the newborn? There is a great demand in the U.S. for adoptable children, and one would hope that there would always be parents married, ready, willing and able to adopt. However, the situation in which there are not ready, willing and able married parents is bound to occur and is discussed in Chapter 11.

F. Divorce.

Nearly 50 percent of marriages today wind up in the divorce courts within ten years. The primary reason is basic money problems brought on by lack of adequate financial planning. This is the worst-case scenario: The sad story begins with a couple's felt need to keep up with their contemporaries, and their going into debt to do it. A young couple wants to get married. One or both of them may already have large credit card debts. According to a study done in 2002 by Nellie Mae, the student-loan financier based in Braintree, Massachusetts, as reported in the Washington Post, the typical student graduating from a four-year college has student loans of nearly $19,000 and credit card debt of about $3,300. The Washington Post further reports that 50 percent of law school graduates have debts of $75,000 or more, and one in five has more than $105,000. The fiancée expects a diamond ring as an engagement gift, which she will show to all of her friends. She doesn't want to show a puny little diamond, and her fiancé doesn't want her to have to, so he buys the largest one he can afford – on credit. Then she wants a nice wedding with all of the trimmings, a considerable expense usually paid by her parents. If not, the couple may have to foot the bill – on credit. Then there is the wedding trip after the ceremony to pay for – on credit.

Their contemporaries all bought an apartment or a house when they were married, and this couple wishes to do so as well, again, to keep up. Easy credit and low mortgage interest rates tempts them, and they do so for a small down payment and large monthly payments on the mortgage-secured note. They also furnish it – on credit. Now, with credit cards maxed out, large mortgage payments, car payments, furniture payments, and monthly installment payments to the jeweler and caterer, their monthly income is pretty well committed. Young couples are encouraged to go into debt like this by easy credit and by government fiscal and monetary policies which result in about a three or four percent annual inflation rate. Couples are aware that they can buy products that they need on credit now and pay less for them (in current dollars) than they would have to pay a year or two later when they might have the cash.

They are able to swing all of this debt as long as both work, but one day she discovers that she is pregnant. When the baby comes, they find themselves in a financial bind. They have limited options. One is an abortion, which would be contrary to the whole purpose of the marriage. Another is to somehow reduce their financial obligations so the mother can stay home with the infant, an option that would be very difficult and, in many cases, impossible to achieve. The third is to put the infant out to day care with the mother continuing to work. As among the three options, day care appears as a no-brainer. They go for it. This decision, although an apparent no-brainer, places great stress on the marriage. Now they are both on the wheel, leading frenetic lives. One feminist fortunate enough to be able to give up her job said as she was giving it up to stay home with the couple's baby, "There just wasn't enough of me to go around."

When two parents work outside the home, they have problems of their own. Not only do they not have enough time for their children, but they also do not have enough time to live their own lives. Frequently, they find themselves rushing around to accomplish all the errands and chores that have to be done. They fall into bed at night exhausted only to get up the next morning and do it all over again, lurching from weekend to weekend. Many parents suffer from stress-related physical and psychological disorders. They are not leading happy lives. Careful financial planning would caution them to use discretion in what they bought on credit and would have allowed her to stay home and raise their baby (or babies) from the outset. It is the couple's fault of course, that they wind up in such a predicament, but easy credit greases the slide into debt, and high government taxes makes it tough to get out.

After a few years of this and fending off creditors, the marriage begins to wear thin and winds up in divorce court. If the children are young, the judge usually gives the mother custody. If they are older, he may award joint custody. This decision for joint custody makes the judge feel Solomon-like and mollifies each parent to some extent, but the children strongly dislike the arrangement, which often causes them to be bounced back and forth like a Ping Pong ball. But what can they do? They are powerless. Women initiate most of the divorce proceedings, and it is they – after the children, of course – who get the short end of the stick. Wives get either sole or joint custody, child support and maybe alimony, but many times they can't collect any or enough of either. Then they are really in a bind without enough money, have to work outside the home and put the children out to day care. Many seek to remarry, but they are not such a good catch because they already have children. Husbands are not much better off because they have lost the opportunity for regular natural sex, and they also often seek to remarry. They too are at a disadvantage in this endeavor because of their existing obligation for child support and (maybe) alimony obligations from their first marriage. Everyone is a loser, but mostly the children.

The situation is bad for many parents now, but it is bound to get worse because it is plain from demographic data as depicted above that more young couples will be taking care of one or more of their aged parents in the future in addition to taking care of their children. And it is not just their own children and parents for whom these people will have to care. Through taxes that must surely increase over time, they will have to support more of <u>other people's</u> children and aged parents, a prison population that is already about two million strong (and growing), and a growing number of other eaters of various kinds. The family is the foundation of our society. Big government has been causing the family as a social institution to decline for some time and, unless something is done, it will continue to decline. A wise man once said, "As goes the family, so goes the nation."

Contrary to what was for years the conventional wisdom, current thinking is that divorce places most children at serious risk. As reported in an October 2, 2000 article in *U.S. News and World Report*, researchers today find that children of divorced parents are more depressed and aggressive towards parents and teachers alike. They are inclined to have more mental and emotional disorders later in life, to abuse drugs, turn to crime, commit suicide, start sexual activity earlier, have more children out of wedlock, are less likely to marry and, when they do, are more likely to divorce. There is evidence that their resentment towards their divorced parents persists for years.

The article also cites the book, *A Generation at Risk* by Paul Amato and Alan Booth, reporting on a study of 2,000 married people, where it was found that 70 percent of American divorces are occurring in low-conflict marriages where the couples don't quarrel often or even disagree much. The article also cited the findings of Linda Waite of the University of Chicago from her analysis of the National Survey of Families and Households that 86 percent of the people surveyed who said they were in bad marriages but stuck it out felt that five years later their marriages were happier.

The article also reported that Judith Wallenstein, in her book *The Unexpected Legacy of Divorce*, based on a long-term study of 131 children of divorce, found that children are not much bothered by their parents quarreling. What they want is for them to stay together.

In view of these down sides to divorce for children, I submit that society would be better off if divorces after the birth of children were almost impossible to come by until the youngest child reached adulthood but were easy to obtain before the birth of a child and after the youngest child reached adulthood.

The law needs to be changed to provide, as a condition for issuing a marriage license, that, once married and at least one child is born, the couple will stay married and provide for their children until the youngest child reaches the age of majority. It should provide for easy divorce at two times after the license is issued: first, before a child is born. Written notification by either partner, duly witnessed, notarized, recorded with the appropriate authority of local government, and published in the local newspaper that the marriage is over is all that should be required. It should provide that property acquired jointly after the marriage be divided equally. Such a provision would give the husband a legal remedy in the event his wife was too frequently averse to having sex or in the event she could not have children. A wife thus divorced who was pregnant would be in a dilemma. Her choices would be to find someone else to marry quickly, terminate the pregnancy by abortion, or continue the pregnancy to term and lose the offspring to adoption. Similarly, if the wife discovered that her husband was unable to provide adequately for the family or if he made too many sexual demands, she also could get relief through easy divorce.

Second, the law should contain a similar provision for easy divorce after the youngest child reaches 18 years of age. The difference in a suitable distribution of assets between those two times would be that, in addition to an equal distribution of property acquired jointly after the marriage, the future income of both parties should also be divided equally when the divorce

112

occurs after the youngest child reached adulthood, an arrangement to exist until one partner or the other dies or until the ex-spouse remarries. Premarital agreements that provided otherwise should be prohibited. No lawyers or courts would be needed either time. Between those times, there would be no divorce at all unless one or both spouses clearly could not perform his or her contract for an extended period of time. As an example, imprisonment of one partner for a felony would be absolute grounds for divorce by the other partner – without costly litigation. Such a change would put thousands of lawyers and judges out of work but would benefit the general populace.

G. Better Schooling.

When people think of labor, they almost automatically think exclusively of manual labor. However, mental labor (thought) is far more valuable than manual (muscle) labor in producing any good or service. One sees that everywhere. For example, the floor sweeper in a small factory does mostly manual labor and very little thinking. He may be paid a salary of $20,000 a year or less. The factory manager, on the other hand, does very little manual labor but does a lot of thinking in planning and directing operations. He may be paid $200,000 or more. The Bureau of the Census estimates that, over their working years, a high school graduate can expect to earn an average of $1.2 million; those with a bachelor's degree, $2.1 million; those with a master's degree, $2.5 million; and those with a professional degree, up to $4.4 million. Thus, educating people and nurturing their ability to think, along with good health, and motivation, is one obvious way of both maximizing the number of producers and minimizing the number of eaters

Public schools have been dragooned into being unwilling baby sitters for students with behavioral and learning problems who impede and disrupt learning of other students. A teacher cannot be effective in an environment that lacks discipline. Teachers have limited authority for maintaining discipline and, when they exercise what authority they do have, are often not backed up by the school principal. Courts need to stay out of school disciplinary problems, and legislatures need to revise current laws, if necessary, to strengthen the position of teachers by eliminating enlarged rights that have come to be enjoyed by students. Teachers need to be able to suspend and expel students for disruptive behavior subject only, perhaps, to review by the school principal.

Courts, perhaps in response to legislation, have afforded students far more rights addressable in court than students used to have. Teachers are reluctant to discipline students because their action may be overturned by the courts or, worse yet, the student may sue them – and win. If teachers are not to be allowed to expel problem children from public schools, measures need to be taken so that they can be placed in other learning environments or put to work at gainful employment. Where they do not already do so, public schools need to include the teaching of various manual skills in the curriculum and to settle expelled students into apprenticeships when possible. Elimination of the minimum wage for student-age workers and allowing child labor for expelled students would facilitate finding work for them.

Another serious shortcoming of public high school curricula today is the failure to teach young women about mothering. This is a skill of the greatest importance to the nation. Another subject that needs to be taught somewhere – and it may not be possible to teach it in public schools – is sex. Young men and women today have no proper way to learn about this critical subject.

Public schools come in for a great deal of criticism these days to the point that many parents search for alternatives in the form of private schools or home schooling. Prospective employers

114

complain that high school graduates have difficulty with mathematics and with understanding instructions. Some cannot read or write very well – or at all. Students entering college, of which there is a very high percentage, frequently have to have remedial training before commencing their college level work. Taxpayers complain that public schools cost too much.

One can easily identify at least some of the reasons that public schools are having these problems. Public schools are required by law to teach all children within an age group ranging generally from six to sixteen whether they are literate in English or not. Commonly, in schools with large non-English speaking populations, the practice has been to teach English as a second language (ESL), and to teach other subjects in the native language of the student. This is expensive, and experience has shown that the practice may actually be detrimental to student learning and to integrating them into the American culture. During the 1920's, many Italians were brought to Western Pennsylvania to work in the coal mines. They were not literate in English at all. No English was spoken in the home. Yet their children attended public schools which taught only in English. They learned English somehow and achieved as well academically as students whose parents were literate in English. So, it can be done. By ballot referendum, California has finally dropped ESL, but implementation is still being litigated in the courts. Other school districts are coming to believe that it is better for the nation and for the non-English-speaking students to drop ESL and may follow California into total immersion curricula where students are taught only in English.

In a misguided effort to avoid damaging the self-image of non-achieving minority students, many schools have resorted to "social promotions"; i.e., promoting students to the next grade whether or not they had mastered the material in their present grade. The extreme result of this practice sometimes has been students graduating from high school who can neither read nor write. The idea of social promotions was to avoid damaging the student's self-esteem by holding him back. Other schools have simplified their curricula so that even the slowest students could pass. Such curricula, known as "dumbed-down curricula," fail to stimulate the interest of even the average student who becomes bored. Academic achievement suffers. The federal government, which has gradually taken a big hand in education over the years through grants, regulations and mandates, has come out recently opposing social promotions and "dumbed-down curricula." With this development, these practices may now be curtailed in some jurisdictions.

Prior to 1954, many students attended schools that were segregated by color. It was in 1954 that Earl Warren wrote the Supreme Court decision in *Brown v. Board of Education of Topeka,* which concluded that such educational facilities for blacks which are separate from whites, even though otherwise equal, are inherently unequal. The means widely selected for implementing this decision was school busing, an expensive solution and one that is time- wasting for students. Instead of busing, perhaps, a better solution would be a return to neighborhood schools with governments subsidizing poorer neighborhood schools (whether white, black, Latino, or mixed) to insure that they were adequately funded for providing a proper level of education.

A carryover from the days when the United States had principally an agrarian economy is the two-and-a-half or three-month summer vacation for public school students. At one time, farmers needed their children at home in the summer to help work the farm. Now that only a very small percentage of the population is engaged in farming, government, parents and, schools have failed to adapt by changing the vacation periods. It is widely known from personal experiences that students forget during the summer vacation a part of what they learned in the preceding school year. Before work for the next grade can start in the fall, teachers often feel compelled to conduct reviews so that students can brush up on at least some subjects. A better way than the long summer vacation often suggested for scheduling vacations for public school students might be to provide five or six two-week vacation periods spaced at approximately equal intervals throughout the calendar year. One of these would undoubtedly be the Christmas vacation and another during the summer for family vacations.

A great deal of what children need to learn should be learned at home, where they spend much more of their lives than they do in school. Some schools have a high proportion of students who come from single-parent broken homes (or homes where the mother has never been married) or homes where both parents work outside the home. Not only do children from such homes not learn as they should at home, but they are also often not adequately motivated in their home environment to learn in school, and they become, instead, discipline problems for schools. Such families are the source of children likely to become eaters as adults. Such young people could often be benefitted by state or federally operated boarding schools where the students live together away from their home environment, study together, work together, sleep together in dormitories, eat the same food together in common cafeterias, wear the same kinds of clothes, have the same teachers and study from the same books –much like *Boy's Town*. No additional government funding for these schools would be required. It would come from other governmental programs terminated as discussed in a later chapter. It might seem that the solutions to these problems would be simple, but they are not because either the government or powerful interest groups, such as the National Education Association, oppose any change.

The Americans with Disabilities Act requires public schools to accept and teach students with disabilities, regardless of how much it may detract from teaching non-disabled students.

The Act needs to be changed to eliminate the requirement for public schools to educate students who are badly disabled mentally or physically. It is impossible for teachers to be effective if they have to teach students who are so incapacitated that they require an inordinate amount of time at the expense of other students in the class. Elimination of this requirement would place a burden — and, sometimes, a huge burden — on the disabled child's parents to provide for his education, but the problem is the parents', not society's, and not the school district's. Parents of such children should seek aid from a church or a charitable institution if needed.

Chapter 6. Minimizing Out-of-Wedlock Pregnancies.

There are only two reasons why unmarried people should not have sex. The first one, as discussed above, is that they are far more likely than a married couple to be unable to support children they beget. The second one is that unmarried couples engaging in sex are thought to be at greater risk of contracting a sexually transmitted (venereal) disease. They may be more likely to but, then again, they may not. If the partners of an unwed couple have vaginal sex with each other but nobody else, they have no more chance of contracting an STD than does a monogamous married couple. Whether married or not, individuals with multiple sex partners are more likely to contract STD than individuals who have single partners. On the other hand, people, whether married or not, would be healthier and happier if they did have sex. Therefore, the aim should be to legitimize out-of-wedlock sex but to prevent out-of-wedlock pregnancies and avoid sexually transmitted diseases.

The possibility of contracting an STD is not an overwhelming reason to abstain from sex when one considers the diseases one can get from eating or drinking. Many more people get sick from eating than they do from having sex. Gravy alone has probably killed more people than all of the STDs combined except AIDS. As to the transmittability of AIDS through vaginal sex, where, unlike anal sex, there is usually no blood involved, the risk of transmission may be grossly overblown. The results of a study were presented a the Eighth Annual Retrovirus Conference in Chicago in February 2001, a study conducted by Johns Hopkins University of 174 sexually monogamous married couples in Rakai, Uganda, engaging in frequent unprotected sex in which one partner had HIV and the other did not. The study concluded that the chance of contracting HIV from a single unprotected natural sexual encounter with an infected person is one in 588. Chances of contracting HIV with *condom-protected* vaginal sex are practically negligible. Of course, one must bear in mind that, unlike other STDs, HIV (which becomes AIDS) is fatal and incurable.

Some of our food – even that which is government inspected – is infected with bacteria. Meat, eggs, fish, fruits, and vegetables must be handled and prepared very carefully to avoid sickness. Many people are allergic to milk, shellfish and wheat, to name a few allergens that can kill or make people extremely ill. The water-born ailments of diarrhea and dysentery cause large numbers of deaths throughout the world, particularly among children. Municipal drinking water in the United States can be hazardous to one's health as well. Consider the problems recently with cryptosporidium in municipal water supplies of several U.S. cities. And this is not to mention the difficulties that people get into from drinking alcoholic beverages. All in all, nearly everything we do in life is fraught with some risk.

A. Celibacy.

The customary way to minimize sexual intercourse among the unwed in the past has been celibacy. This way used to work and work quite well. Fathers' advice to sons was to keep your penis in your pants. Mothers' advice to daughters was to keep your panties up and your knees together. It worked because there was a powerful social stigma against out-of-wedlock pregnancies. Unfortunately, the moralizing that usually came with these admonitions often resulted in shame and guilt about sex that continued on into the married lives of men and women.

Parents did not want their teenage sons and daughters to create pregnancy situations because the parents had already reared or were still rearing children of their own. They did not want – and, in many cases, could not afford – to raise their daughter's children.

We talk about "teenage pregnancies." Churches stigmatized *any* extramarital sex (fornication), and most jurisdictions had laws to make it illegal. Others deplored the promiscuity they feared would result if extramarital sex was not banned. What society really needed to oppose was not just teenage pregnancies or extramarital sex but *any* pregnancies (married or not) where the couple were not likely to be able to support their offspring because, in those cases, society would have to do it and did not want to.

It used to be that, if a young unmarried woman became pregnant, her life was ruined. She was ostracized, ridiculed, and talked about. Her child was a bastard. She had to drop out of school. Knowing this, unmarried women were reluctant to have sex. Young men, realizing it also, were reluctant to press them to do so. The best that her parents could do for a daughter pregnant out of wedlock was to ship her off to live with a relative in a distant city until the baby was born and there adopt the baby out. If the lid were kept on tight enough, she could return home and nobody was the wiser. Next best was the shotgun wedding. In such a wedding, the couple was forced to marry. Parents had to help out financially until the young man could support a family. Abortions at that time were a poor option. Physicians could lose their license to practice medicine if they were caught performing an abortion and might even be criminally prosecuted. It was nearly impossible to find a reputable physician who would do one. An abortion performed by a quack with a wire coat hanger in the back room of a seedy hotel was a dangerous alternative, sometimes leading to sterility or the death of the mother.

Today, the social stigma against out-of-wedlock pregnancies has disappeared. Why did the social stigma disappear? It disappeared because governments began providing the support for mothers and their offspring who were otherwise without support. Laws were passed and funds were budgeted. The arrangement gives the appearance that government is footing the bills and society (the taxpayer) is off the hook. Of course, society is still providing the support for these children and their mothers who are either not married at all or are married to husbands unable or unwilling to support them, but it is hard for taxpayers to see the connection between the increased taxes they have to pay and the support payments. Consequently, society no longer condemns out-of-wedlock births.

It is quite a hardship on young people to be asked to forego natural sex until they are able to support children, if one considers that the appetite for sex is a natural one the same as appetites for food or drink. Consider this: We have to eat and drink to live. And why do we live? We live to achieve the three purposes of life: namely, to procreate, to be happy, and to improve ourselves so we can cross over the bar as better souls than we were as born into this life. But we don't eat and drink merely to sustain life. If we ate simply to stay alive, we would subsist very well and very cheaply on a diet of corn, beans and greens, and would be healthier for it. We eat for pleasure, to make ourselves happy. One can tell this from the type of foods that we eat; namely, such tasty foods as hamburgers, fries, ice cream, candy, and pastries. One can also tell that we don't eat simply to live by noting that about 65 percent of the population is overweight and that about half of these are obese.

It's the same with drink. All we need in the way of liquids is water, but we drink a host of other kinds of beverages including soft drinks, alcoholic beverages, juices, tea, coffee, and cocoa. Why? Because it gives us pleasure to do so. Drinking liquids besides water makes us happy. They make us feel good. Would parents ask sons and daughters to forgo all kinds of food and drink except the most basic until they were able to support children? Not likely, but they do ask them to forgo natural sex until then.

There are two differences between the appetites for food and drink on the one hand and the appetite for natural sex on the other. The first difference is that, unlike food and drink, sex is not necessary for life, but it is necessary for procreation, which is one of the three purposes we live for. As with food and drink, people don't engage in sex just for procreation. If that was the sole reason, people might engage in sex only a few times in a lifetime for the purpose of begetting children. Rather, most people engage in sex often and for pleasure the same as we do with eating and drinking. It makes us happy.

The second difference is that satisfaction of the appetites for food and drink, on the one hand, requires only substances, but satisfaction of the appetite for natural sex, on the other hand, requires the consent and, preferably, the cooperation of another person of the opposite sex. That consent is sometimes not easy to come by. Because appetites for food and drink are easily satisfied in this country, the appetite for natural sex is the primary motivating force for most men and many women because it is not so easy to arrange natural sexual satisfaction..

There are no known studies to support the following thoughts, but we know that substitution exists for at least one appetite, and that is for people trying to quit smoking. They try subconsciously to satisfy the acquired appetite for nicotine with the natural appetite for food. Consequently, they overeat and get fat. It works the other way, too. People who are overweight often take up smoking to curb their appetite for food. Lovers often address one another in food terms, such as honey, sweetie-pie or some dish. Men sometimes refer to women they are escorting as arm candy. Photos of females are sometimes referred to as cheesecake and males as beef cake.

Binge drinking and the use of drugs, particularly by men, may be other examples of subconscious efforts to substitute satisfaction of an acquired appetite (for alcohol and drugs) for satisfaction of the natural appetite for sex. A high proportion of young men are prone to driving cars fast and sometimes recklessly and performing dangerous stunts on skis, skateboards, and the like. The adrenaline rush they get from such dangerous activities may well serve as a substitute for the stimulation achievable through natural sex. It is surprising how such men, when the opportunity for regular natural sex is available through marriage, settle down and become faithful husbands and good providers. Researchers have long suspected that the high level of testosterone in males – which is largely responsible for fighting, competing, and mating – decreases when men marry and settle down. A recent study conducted at Harvard University by a professor and several of his students using saliva tests has confirmed that married men have markedly lower testosterone levels than single males. Doubtless, this is a result of married men having access to natural sex on a regular basis. It seems logical that streets and highways would be safer for everyone, and far fewer young, unmarried men would be maimed and killed by their own acts of derring-do if they had regular access to natural sex.

We know that serious physiological – and, perhaps, psychological – consequences stem from a starvation diet whereby sufficient food is denied a person for an extended period of time. Very likely, the same is true when a person suffers severe but not fatal dehydration for an extended period of time as when a person is adrift at sea in an open boat. Are there such consequences when a person voluntarily or involuntarily suffers extended sex deprivation? Could it be, for example, that the reason women are more prone to rheumatoid arthritis than are men is because they are more prone to repressing their sexual appetites than are men? Doing so is natural for women because they suffer more severe consequences from sex gone wrong (unwanted pregnancy) than do men? Are unsatisfied appetites for sex the cause for the high incidence of depression, suicide, and attempted suicide among teenagers? Here again, the rate of attempted suicide among female high school students (10.9 percent) is nearly double that of male high school students (5.7 percent).

People are born with a natural appetite for sex, and it remains with us, to one degree of intensity or another, for the rest of our lives. The appetite for sex becomes particularly keen after puberty but is evident also in young children. Witness this: An 11-year-old Swiss American boy was arrested for sexually molesting his 5-year-old sister because a neighbor in Golden, Colorado, reported that she witnessed him touching the sister "inappropriately." Get that. Where could an 11-year-old brother be touching his 5-year-old sister inappropriately? Even if he was touching her genitals, what harm could that do if he wasn't hurting her? Both of them probably found the experience gratifying although neither could have been old enough to experience an orgasm. The Swiss parents promptly took their family and left the country saying they feared that Colorado authorities would take their children away from them as unfit parents. One has to wonder about the Colorado law, Colorado authorities – and the meddling neighbor.

Similar cases involving juvenile sex are not uncommon. Another case was reported from York Haven, Pennsylvania, where six out of a "ring" of seventeen children were charged in juvenile court with rape, involuntary deviate sexual intercourse, and indecent assault because they taught each other to have – and were having – sex. The chief of police there said that these kids knew what they were doing wasn't right. One must wonder exactly what all it was they had been doing that wasn't right, and was anybody harmed? One 16-year-old girl who admitted to having sex with an eleven-year old boy was convicted of rape because the difference between their ages was more than four years. What harm could these two young people engaging in sex have done to the eleven-year old? STD? Hardly. However, the conviction of rape will do the young woman a great deal of harm.

125

Because the sexual appetite is strong in the majority of the population, men and women are going to engage in sexual intercourse from time to time no matter what. We know that. The Associated Press reported on a study conducted by researchers at Child Trends based on a national survey that tracked 8,000 teens for five years from 1997. The study revealed that about one-third of high school freshmen and three-fifths of seniors had already had sex. Contrary to conventional thinking, sex did not take place in the back seat of a car. More than half of the time, it took place in their family home of one of the partners. Also, contrary to conventional thinking, it did not take place in the afternoon between the time they got home from school and the time their parents got home from work. Over 40 percent of the teens had their first sexual encounter between 10 P.M. and 7 A.M. Another 28 percent had it in the evening between 6 and 10 P.M..

The appetite for sex among men and women is probably greater today than it used to be. The reason is because sexual appetites are continually whetted by pictures of semi-nude women in seductive poses and gyrations. On prime time television and in the movies we are treated to views of scantily-clad women cavorting about, performing maneuvers that could once be seen only in a burlesque theater. Women's everyday, party, and beach clothing is generally much more revealing than it ever was before.

Not only are the sexual appetites of men and women whetted almost constantly these days, but the period of enforced abstinence from natural sex has gotten longer. In 1970, the median age at which a man married for the first time was 23 years for men and 21 for women Today, it is 27 years for men and 25 years for women –13 or 14 years past the age of puberty.

Celibacy never would have been an effective way of limiting out-of-wedlock sex if it were not for masturbation. The natural way for sex is vaginal sex with a man's penis in a woman's vagina. Society has engineered its rules so that the only acceptable way to satisfy one's sexual appetite in the natural way is within the bonds of matrimony. Since most young people are unable financially to accommodate to matrimony, they are left with the poor alternative of masturbation as the most common way of relieving themselves unless they are willing to break society's rules. Strangely, some parents discourage even this benign practice by warning the masturbator that he would die, go blind, et cetera.

The situation for men is worse than for women because men have to contend with semen pressure which builds up constantly and must be relieved. Testicles become engorged and the prostate gland swells causing continual discomfort. The story goes that a young man's parents sent him to a psychologist to seek help with some of his socially unacceptable behavior. The psychologist gave him a little verbal quiz to focus on the problem:

Psychologist: "You have been down to the airport and watched a large airliner take off; What did that remind you of?"

Young Man: " Reminded me of sex."

Psychologist: "Uh huh, you have watched white clouds drifting by in a blue sky on a warm summer day, haven't you? What did that picture bring to mind?"

Young man: "Sex."

Psychologist: "I see. When you see a leaf falling from a tree in the autumn, what does that make you think of?"

Young man: "It makes me think of sex."

Psychologist (in some exasperation): "How could all of these different scenes make you think of sex?"

Young man: "Sex is all I think about."

In summary, celibacy is not effective in today's social environment, and improvements in contraceptives have rendered celibacy largely unnecessary for men and women who are educated in their use. However, as unrealistic as the policy of abstinence until marriage is, the federal government continues to push it with bloc grants to states. Preaching celibacy alone is not enough to discourage sexual intercourse among the unwed and, thus, improve the producer/eater ratio. Other steps, such as reinstating single-sex educational institutions and modifying women's dress, would help.

B. Single-sex Educational Institutions.

One of the least intrusive ways of stemming the inflow of eaters into the population is to discourage sex between males and females when they are young and unable financially to support a family. If young men and women don't get together so often, it stands to reason that they won't have sex so often and won't produce so many babies out of wedlock. When young men and women are together, they excite one another in a sexual way. One can at times almost feel the electricity in the air when young men and women get together in a social situation and their gonads are aroused. So, one way to minimize sexual relations is to keep young males and females apart. Preparatory schools and colleges often used to be single-sex. Most such schools – even the military academies – are now coed in this country, having succumbed to pressure from the federal government for eliminating segregation of the sexes, which is considered to be a form of illegal discrimination outlawed by Title IX of the Civil Rights Act of 1964. Only lately, the George W. Bush administration has taken a stance somewhat different from the federal government's previous position, and has introduced regulations to encourage single-sex education in public schools. Other countries have continued to separate the sexes in schools, and some religious sects in this country continue to discourage dancing and other activities which bring the sexes together.

C. Constraints on Women's Dress.

Another means of deterring sexual relations used in other countries is to constrain the way women dress. A radical example of such constraint is the long, loose-fitting dress, veil and head covering worn by Muslim women when they appear in public. Dressed in this way, it is not possible for anyone to tell whether females are old, young, shapely, beautiful, or homely and thus, their appearance does not excite men sexually.

Contrast such dress with that of young women in this country and many other Christian industrialized countries. Women's shoes often have high heels, which accentuate the curves of their bodies in an erotic way. Before 1926, brassieres were simply cloth bands which bound a woman's breasts against her chest. Then, Ida Rosenthal, a Russian immigrant, invented and patented the now-popular cup brassiere which did for women's breasts what high heels did for their legs and torsos. Women regularly show not only their faces, but also a great deal of skin elsewhere. Among young women, short, tight dresses are de rigueur. Tops are often very decolleté with arms, back, belly, and much of the breasts exposed. After a bikini wax job to remove excess hair, much of the pubic area may be exposed as well. In fact, women may decently expose all parts of their bodies these days except their anuses, vulvae and nipples, and even some of these are sometimes exposed without serious social repercussions. This is the last shred that remains of a decency standard for women's dress. Such lack of attire excites men and often leads to pressure for sexual relations. So, the manner of dress in this country is no deterrent to sexual relations; it actually promotes it and is counterproductive to stemming the flow of out-of-wedlock births.

It is unlikely that a dress code or decency standard for women's dress could be legislated anywhere in this country at this time. Feminists could be expected to vehemently oppose it as an erosion of the power they have acquired in recent years. Women have two sources of power. One source is the physical attraction they have for men, the same way a flame attracts moths. Men cannot resist. Monica Lewinsky snapped her thong and Bill Clinton succumbed. The sexual attraction of males to females exists throughout the animal kingdom. Without this attraction, most animal life would have long ago ceased to exist. Women, of course, have been fully aware of their attraction since the time of Cleopatra and before. They enhance it with numerous kinds of cosmetics, perfume, and dress – or lack thereof. The other source of power women have is their political or voting power as a majority group. They could not be expected to give up easily any part of the power they have acquired.

In some jurisdictions, it might be possible to enact legislation denying the protection of law to women alleging sexual harassment when, at the time of an alleged offense, they were wearing high heels, tight-fitting clothes, diaphanous clothes, or clothes that did not cover their arms above the elbows, their torso below the clavicle bones, front and back (nursing mothers excepted), and their legs above the knees. If such legislation were enacted, it should also provide that women who allowed themselves to be photographed in such attire would be denied the protection of these laws, as long as the photographs were in the public domain. Those individuals photographing women wearing such attire and those publishing the images should also be subject to punishment as well. Such laws would encourage more modest dress among women, would have the beneficial effect of decreasing the sexual excitement of men who saw them, and would strike a blow to the pornography production industry in this country.

D. Contraception.

1. The Rhythm Method.

The Roman Catholic Church favors the rhythm method of preventing conception; that is, sex should be avoided during that time of the month when the female is ovulating and fertile. The problem is that it is hard to tell with any degree of accuracy when a female is ovulating or when she is about to ovulate. Having sex may possibly bring on ovulation early. She may experience her greatest desire for sex during ovulation. Also, in the heat of passion, couples may act regardless of the time of the month. This is probably one reason why good Catholic couples often have large families. This method provides no protection against STD and very little against conception.

2. Sponges and Diaphrams.

A third way to prevent conception is mechanically with a barrier sponge or diaphragm inserted into the vagina to cover the cervix at the base of the uterus. Used with a spermatocide, they prevent the sperm from entering the female's uterus. Both are fairly effective in preventing conception, but are of no value in preventing STD.

3. Condoms.

Male latex condoms are widely used as an effective means of preventing conception and the only effective means of preventing transmission of sexual disease. Consumers Union tested 30 condoms and reported in the June 1999 issue of its *Consumer Report*s magazine. They found that the quality of condoms tested this time to be vastly improved over those tested in 1995. Only two of the thirty condoms tested – a *Trojan* model and a *Durex* model – failed the basic test this time. Regular, extra strength, thin, and spermicidal condoms all performed about the same. They found that condoms older than the expiration date on the package may have lost enough elasticity to cause them to fail. Condoms used scrupulously will allow, perhaps, two or three women out of a hundred to become pregnant over a year. Condoms shield against all diseases transmitted by the sex organs, but are of no protection against herpes if it is transmitted by skin contact <u>around</u> the sex organs, usually through visible open sores. A study reported recently in *The New England Journal of Medicine* showed that the chance of passing herpes to a partner was 3.6 percent among 741 couples who used condoms or abstained from sex during an outbreak. The problem with male condoms is one of educating people to use them. To be effective, condoms must be used properly and used every time. Female condoms have not caught on very well so far.

4. The "Pill" and Implants.

The most common method used by females in the United States for preventing conception is "the pill" taken orally every day. Another is the use of slow-release contraceptive rods (Norplant, recently taken off the market), implanted surgically under the skin on the female's upper arm, which slowly release a steady dose of contraceptive hormones for a period of five years. There is a skin patch effective for a week, and a ring inserted in the vagina effective for a month. All of these perform much the same way as pills but avoid the necessity for pill-taking every day. These methods are very effective (perhaps 97 or 98 percent) and seem to have minimum adverse effect on the health of the female. Since these measures are taken before a sexual encounter, they are not subject to being overlooked or ignored in the heat of passion.

They do not shield against STD. For the most part, all of these methods for preventing conception are approved by the people of the United States — good Catholics, perhaps, excepted.

5. Intrauterine Devices.

According to the United Nations, IUD's are the most popular temporary contraception in the world. The devices appear to be very effective in preventing conception, are reasonably safe, but are of no effect in preventing STD. At one time, intrauterine devices implanted in the cervix of the female uterus were more widely used in the United States than they are today. One of these devices was the then-popular Dalkon Shield, the use of which in the 1970s caused serious problems, including sterility and death for some users. Multiple filaments attached to the device were thought to be the culprit allowing bacteria into the uterus. Its manufacture and sale were discontinued. There are several other brands of IUDs without filaments on the market in the United States, but they currently represent only a tiny percentage of the contraceptive market. This may change. A study of IUDs use in Mexico, published in the *New England Journal of Medicine* in August 2001, and funded by the National Institutes of Health and the Agency for International Development, found that women who were never pregnant suffered little risk from their use. They provide cheap, effective, permanent-until-removed, maintenance-free protection against an unwanted pregnancy. They provide no protection against STD.

6. Sterilization.

A fourth way is to prevent conception surgically by either tying off or cutting the fallopian tubes of the female, or by tying off or cutting the male vas deferens tubes. When the female tubes are interdicted, sperm cells deposited in the female's vagina have no way to reach the eggs in her ovaries. When the male tubes are interdicted, the sperm cells have no way of traveling from the testicles to the penis and thence to the vagina. This is the most effective and also the most common method for preventing conception in the world today, but it is not for anyone who may later want to have children because it will likely be impossible to reconnect the tubes. Once sterilized, it is usually for a lifetime. It is very effective for preventing pregnancies, but is no protection against STD.

E. Abortion.

If conception is not prevented, then the next way to reduce the number of out-of-wedlock births is by aborting pregnancies, which means killing either the embryo or fetus, depending upon the stage of the pregnancy at which it is done. Abortions are a big emotional, moral, and political issue in this country. We have the "Pro-lifers" and the "Pro-choicers" with strongly held opposing views. Near-term abortions, where the fetus's brain is sucked out and its skull collapsed just before birth, are by far the most objectionable. Other means, such as injecting saline into the uterus of the pregnant mother or rupturing the amniotic sac sometime during the pregnancy, do not appear to be as objectionable, but any means employed by physicians to abort a fetus is so objectionable to some Pro- lifers that they are willing to stand outside abortion clinics picketing them in all kinds of weather. A few are so passionately opposed to abortions that they have bombed and burned clinics and killed physicians who perform abortions. Whether Pro-lifers would feel so strongly about "morning after" pills is uncertain. In essence, "morning after" pills are large doses of "the pill" that the potential mother can take within a few days after having unprotected sex to avoid pregnancy. Whether or not abortions are morally wrong and whether or not they should be illegal hinges on the answer to a number of questions discussed in Chapter 11.

F. Sex Education.

Questions of even very young children about their bodies and sex need to be answered early, truthfully, frankly, and openly. No more stories about the stork having brought you. Puberty is the most critical time. The bodies of young men and women entering puberty are flooded with new and powerful hormones. Radical changes take place in their bodies at that time, and their appetite for sex is kindled. They need to understand what is going on. Without knowledge about sex and the troubles that unprotected sexual activities can get them into, these young people are certain to encounter more difficulties than they would if they were educated about sex. It is all very well to counsel adolescents simply not to have sex, but they are going to have it, and they need to know about the subject. Churches, as well as schools, need to take a hand in an effort to change views about the morality of sex. Parents and parent-teacher associations should promote the education of young men and women with regard to sex.

Women bear and rear the children, and it is, therefore, their natural right to decide which male (or males) can mate with them. That is why rape is such a serious crime. It deprives women of this right. Were it not for deprivation of that right, rape would be nothing more than simple assault and battery. Absent forcible rape, women who are educated about sex can have complete control over whether or not they become pregnant. That is why it is more important that women be educated about sex and the various means of birth control than it is for men.

Educating young men and women about sex is a task many believe to be the province of the parents, but parents often feel uncomfortable in teaching their children about sex. One reason for their discomfort may be because they themselves don't really know much about the subject. Their parents never taught them. What they know – or think they know – they learned from a friend, an older sibling, or by trial and error. Parents who wish to educate their children about sex ought to be sure that they themselves are well enough versed on the subject beforehand. Perhaps, *they* should take a course or two on the subject before they start. Another problem that parents may have is unwarranted carryover feelings of guilt and shame as a consequence of their parents and the church moralizing on the subject. It is difficult to be objective with such feelings.

Consider this: children have no opportunity to learn about sex by parental example. They see their parents performing almost every bodily function and learn from them by just watching. Children, from when they are very young, see their parents play, eat, drink, sleep, walk, shower, bathe, and occasionally defecate and urinate. The most enlightened parents sometimes even permit their children to remain in the delivery room to witness the birth of their siblings. Show me parents, however, who would permit a child to watch them conceiving a sibling!

However it is done or whoever does it, the veil needs to be lifted from sex one way or another, at least by the time children reach puberty. Young men and women today learn about sex the same way their parents did, from their peers and older siblings, much of it probably wrong. Such is not a really satisfactory way to educate young people. It's much like a person who teaches himself to play golf. Once the neo-golfer begins to take lessons from a pro, the first thing he has to do, as a rule, is unlearn what he has already learned, because it is wrong.

The media and the Internet have done a great deal in recent years to liberalize the attitudes of people about sex. Sex is more explicit on television and in the movies than ever before.

However, curricula are needed that cover every aspect of a person's own sex and relationships with the opposite sex. Some schools are working at this already, but the major problem will be in finding knowledgeable teachers willing to teach the subject, and in protecting them from the opprobrium they would be sure to suffer in today's cultural environment. Young people need to be taught objectively about changes that have taken place or will take place in their bodies, about conception and birth, about sexually transmitted diseases, about various means of avoiding conception and venereal disease, and about abortions. They need to be taught all facets of sexual relations; foreplay; examination of the sexual organs; examination, application, and removal of a condom; and the various positions for performing the act. They can see much of this on television, in the movies, and on the Internet. They need to know about the spiritual values of sex and emotional effects. Parents need to be involved in this as well as churches. Some parents may not want their young men and women to have this kind of information, but it is simply a truism to say that knowledge is better than ignorance. A study conducted recently by Emory University in Atlanta, Georgia, that reviewed 44 studies involving 35,000 teenagers found that contrary to common concerns, those attending sex education classes started having sex later, used condoms more, and had fewer sex partners.

Probably the best thing that a mother can do for her daughter to help her avoid unwanted pregnancies and sexually transmitted disease is to make sure that she attends a good, comprehensive course on sex that emphasizes monogamous or near monogamous sexual relationships and the use of condoms. If daughters were fitted with IUDs, they plus the condoms – if the daughter can be persuaded to insist on their use – will practically guarantee against unwanted pregnancies. A monogamous or near monogamous sexual relationship plus the regular use of condoms will almost certainly prevent sexually transmitted disease.

Parents should allow their teenagers to have a bolt on the inside of their bedroom door for privacy and should try not to look shocked when, for the first time, the teenager comes downstairs for breakfast – with the significant other of the opposite sex. Let young people learn. Let them make their own informed decisions. Young people will be happier, and many unwanted pregnancies and much venereal disease will be prevented. Births of potential eaters will be curtailed.

G. Prostitution.

Another means to deter out-of-wedlock conception is to legalize and destigmatize the oldest profession of them all, prostitution. Prostitution is illegal in most jurisdictions. Legalized and destigmatized prostitution is especially important to a country like the United States where the media constantly bombards the male population with pictures of females in erotic poses and dressed in scanty and seductive clothing. Many women on the street and in the work place actually dress this way, causing sexual excitement among the males exposed. Such males sometimes go on the prowl. Many marry to get regular sex before they are financially able to support a wife and children. Some harass women. Some rape. It is much better to have satisfactory legal outlets for male sexual appetites.

There are many men in this country who cannot – and never will be able to – support a family. Prisons are full of them. These men are frequently from single-parent, broken or dysfunctional families who, for whatever reason, did not receive the support and encouragement they needed to do well in school. They either didn't graduate from high school at all or they graduated without marketable skills. Once they left school, their parent(s) no longer wanted to and may not have been able to continue supporting them, and they really had no legitimate way to support themselves. So they sought to provide for themselves in ways frowned upon by society and wound up in prison. Others tried to support themselves in a legal way, but that was not at a very high level. Lawn maintenance companies, for example, are often staffed with such men. It doesn't require a great deal of effort or skill to provide the basic needs of a single man in terms of food, clothing and shelter, but if a man wants to have natural sex today in this country legally, he has to get married. Men lacking marketable skills cannot afford to get married, but they still need a legal outlet for their natural sex appetites. With such an outlet, many would be content to live out their lives unmarried and supporting themselves at the low income levels they are able to command.

The practice of engaging in sex for money is a profession which has flourished for thousands of years and flourishes yet today even in jurisdictions where its practice is punishable by law. The practice in the United States today takes two primary forms: streetwalkers and call girls. More of it is practiced under the guise of massage parlors, escort services, and bar girls. Women in the profession working on the streets have to practice it in the most dangerous ways. They have to get into a car with a man they don't know and go somewhere with him alone to have sex. They are extremely vulnerable to injury or murder. The same is true with call girls. Both are often victimized by pimps who exploit them, sometimes brutalize them and introduce them to illegal, habit-forming drugs. In the enforcement of laws against prostitution, the police are constantly harassing and arresting them, and the courts regularly fine or jail them.

One must ask logically why the practice is considered to be immoral and illegal. For mainly one reason: Nations historically have had as a goal increasing the size of the population. Since practitioners of sex for money do not have many babies, their having sex did not further the national goal. Likewise, males with access to regular sex outside of marriage are less likely to enter into marriage with all of its obligations of providing for children than are those who do not have such access. However, laws and mores need to change because increasing the size of the population is not the goal of most nations anymore. Then there is the matter of sexually transmitted disease. There was once (much more so than today) a real danger of contracting trichinosis from eating pork. Making it immoral for Jews and Muslims to eat pork was an effective way to prevent the faithful from contracting this dreadful ailment. Similarly, at one time, a person was more likely to acquire a venereal disease by having sex for money than by having sex for love inside or outside of marriage. Is it not likely that making it immoral to have sex for money was a way for protecting the faithful from contracting venereal disease? Whether or not there is a greater danger of STD today one way or the other is uncertain.

Individuals are often inculcated with the idea that there is something deeply immoral and prurient about the practice of exchanging sex for money. Much of this attitude is likely a carryover from the Puritans who believed that nearly anything pleasurable, was *ipso facto*, sinful. A case was reported in the newspapers a few years ago about a father who took his son to a bordello to learn about and to have natural sex. Governmental authorities found out about it, arrested the father and charged him with contributing to the delinquency of a minor.

What is so sacred about a woman's body that she cannot use it to make a living? Thousands of athletes, male and female, use their bodies in professional sports to earn princely salaries. Some of their bodies are badly beaten up playing sports, suffering far more damage than a woman legally engaging in sex for money is likely to endure. The vagina is a muscular organ and, like most muscles, may actually benefit from exercise. Does the frequent use of the organ impair her ability later on to bear healthy children? There is no evidence that it does, unless she contracts a sexually transmitted disease which goes uncured. Many single mothers, now eking out a living for their children on welfare or on low-paying jobs, could provide handsomely for them if she wished to do so and if she could enter the profession as a moral and legal enterprise. Such mothers could convert from a current status as eaters to one of producers.

Politically correct terms need to be encouraged because of the negative connotations associated with present terminology. Pejorative terms for these institutions, like "cat houses, brothels, bordellos, bawdy houses, houses of ill-repute, and sporting houses" should be dropped in favor of the more acceptable and politically correct term of Friendship Houses. Employees there should be termed as hostesses instead of whores, hookers, prostitutes, harlots, street walkers, women of the night, and the like. Such changes would be in keeping with other politically correct changes in terminology such as for homosexuals who were once called homos, lesbians, or queers but are now called gays, an appellation more to their liking. Afro-Americans have likewise benefitted from the use of politically correct terminology.

Churches should recognize changes in the national goal and the changed likelihood of contracting a venereal disease in a Friendship House, and should take the lead in changing mores to destigmatize the profession much in the same way as they have done with gambling (which is not a natural appetite at all but one *acquired* by some who gamble). Churches now engage in gambling (bingo) themselves and think it to be okay. In light of recent sex scandals, the Roman Catholic Church which insists that its priests do not marry should welcome and embrace an opportunity for them to have natural sex morally and legally outside of marriage. Generally, it should not be much of a stretch for churches to destigmatize the practice of sex for money.

Some state governments have made an easy transition from gambling being a crime to practicing it themselves (state lotteries, casinos, racetracks, slot machines). States should have no more difficulty with legalizing the oldest profession. Zoning laws need to be changed so that Friendship Houses can be located in any area of the jurisdiction where law, medicine, and dentistry can be practiced. If the profession and its practitioners were legalized, women engaged in the profession could practice it in such houses in safety and comfort instead of in cheap motel rooms, alleys, and the back seats of cars. They would enjoy legal safeguards against long working hours and unsanitary conditions. They could be protected from having to drink or use drugs with their customers. Friendship Houses could be required to make condoms mandatory as a means of minimizing sexually transmitted disease. Practitioners would be protected from having to work without them. The state could require regular medical testing of practitioners. Friendship Houses could better control their clientele. Their right to refuse customers could be protected and they would, of course, have the right to go to the police. These establishments could be organized into partnerships and corporations, licensed and taxed like any other profession. Jurisdictions receive no money from the profession now, except the little they collect through fines. Sometimes, these women are jailed for practicing their profession; then, society pays for their room, board, and medical care while they are incarcerated.

Women engaged in the profession render a valuable service by satisfying the natural appetites of men and should be under the protection of the police and the courts, just like any other business or profession, instead of being an object of harassment. They would provide a means for young, unmarried men to reduce their testosterone levels naturally. Most states have laws that penalize people for driving with elevated blood alcohol levels. None of the states have laws penalizing people for driving with elevated testosterone levels, although one is just about as dangerous as the other. If states had such laws, some young unmarried men might not be allowed to drive at all.

The profession has been legalized in the country of Netherlands (for one) and in the state of Nevada. Available information indicates that the practice is working out very well in both places. It should work out well anywhere. The press reported in 1999 that the Czech government planned to legalize prostitution so that it could tax prostitutes' earnings. The New Zealand tax collection agency also was seeking ways to collect taxes on the $240 million it estimates New Zealanders spend on sex.

Section B. Reducing the Size of Eater Pools.

Minimizing the number of eaters at the source and in the pipeline is a much easier objective to accomplish and will have fewer social repercussions than reducing the number of eaters in the existing eater pools. More drastic measures, sure to meet with vigorous resistance, are needed to accomplish the latter objective. However, measures for reducing the number of eaters at the source and in the pipeline will take years to produce results, but results from efforts to reduce the number of eaters in currently existing pools could be achieved much quicker.

Chapter 7. Immigrants.

Control of immigration is the province of the federal government and subject to federal law. The United States government allows a certain amount of immigration and also allows legal immigrants to become citizens after certain conditions are met. Besides the immigrants entering the country legally, there is also a large influx of illegal immigrants. Illegal immigration, aside from being a violation of federal law, is a mixed blessing at best, because many of such immigrants have no skills and, especially in times of high unemployment, become a burden on welfare programs.

A. Freeloaders.

There are about 30 million immigrants living in the U.S. who entered legally, and there are another estimated 8 million illegals living here, 40 percent of whom entered legally for a limited period of time and then just stayed on. In years prior to 1965, the immigrants came from European countries. These days, the overwhelming majority of legal immigrants come from Mexico, other Latin American countries and Asia. It was a change to the immigration law in 1965 that triggered this transformation when Congress abolished immigration quotas, which favored European countries, and made family unification the primary criterion for admittance. The amended law allows immigrants already in the United States to bring in their relatives who, in turn, could bring in more relatives. Consequently, the U.S. has been admitting as many as one million immigrants a year, so that now one in every ten residents is foreign-born.

A Census Bureau Report issued in 2002 profiling the foreign born population in the U.S. in 1997, found that about 25 percent of immigrants receive some form of income-related federal assistance. Immigrants have for years been eligible for aid under Supplemental Security Income (SSI), food stamps, Medicaid and more than 50 smaller programs. That is a big reason why so many immigrants settle in the U.S. SSI is a major lure. Congress enacted SSI in 1972 to provide monthly cash payments to elderly, blind and disabled persons and the program has grown steadily.

About two-thirds of the 915,000 legal immigrants admitted to the U.S. in 1996 either had no job or did not report one. They come to the U.S. for a better life, and welfare provides it. Whether legal or illegal, most immigrants choose states in which to settle at least partially because of the state's beneficent welfare programs – California, New York, Texas, and Florida. (The value of the welfare programs in California and New York exceeds the average per-capita income in Mexico.) Louisiana and Alabama, also close to Mexico geographically, deny welfare benefits to non-citizens, and those states do not have many immigrants.

According to an August 1997 article in Investor's Business Daily, based on data from the General Accounting Office and the Census Bureau, more and more elderly immigrants are coming to the U.S. and drawing from generous welfare programs, including

Medicaid, housing, and Supplemental Security Income. They come sponsored by their children already in this country who are required to sign a pledge that the immigrant will not become a public charge in the U.S., but the courts have held that the pledge is not binding. More than a third of immigrants over 65 who had been sponsored for entry between 1980 and 1987 were on welfare in 1990. One study shows that each immigrant who comes here at age 60 costs taxpayers an average of nearly $150,000 during his lifetime. The Congressional Budget Office estimated in 1997 that over the next five years, the federal cost of elderly immigrants on SSI and Medicaid would total more than $7 billion.

A Congressional Budget Office paper published in February 1995 said that in 1993, 29 percent of those 65 and older receiving SSI payments were immigrants, but of those recipients in that age bracket not qualifying for Social Security (SS) – that is, hadn't worked here and paid into SS long enough to qualify – 63 percent were immigrants.

Immigrants from Latin America (legal and illegal), who are almost always poor are entitled to welfare benefits. California passed Proposition 187 to deny benefits to illegal aliens, but the courts struck it down as discriminatory. Steven A. Camarato, reporting on a study conducted by the Center for Immigration Studies (CIS), based on Census Bureau's Current Population Survey for March 1998, noted that the percentage of immigrant households on welfare is 30 percent to 50 percent higher than that of natives. New immigrant families, particularly those from Latin America, receive more in government services than they pay in taxes because they have more school-aged children and require more educational services than do other households. In 1995, one billion dollars in benefits went to children born to persons living illegally in the U.S.

The Immigration and Naturalization Service (INS) has the right to deport legal immigrants who are "public charges", but the INS has been reluctant to enforce this right, partly because Congress has not defined public charges and partly because of political pressure on the INS not to do it. The question here is, do the American people wish to continue providing welfare for aliens? I submit that they do not. I submit that Americans are proud to live in a country known as the land of the free, but that they do not wish it to be the land of the free lunch for the world.

Another argument for curtailing immigration is the difficulty the United States is experiencing in assimilating so many ethnic groups, nationalities, and religious groups. Assimilation of immigrants today into a culturally and linguistically unified nation, as the United States has been so successful in doing over the course of its history, is now more difficult – and, perhaps, impossible. Changes that have increased the difficulty are abandonment of the work ethic for a kind of a quasi-welfare state; acceptance of multi-cultures over a primary mono-culture; and multilingualism instead of insistence upon English as the common language. It is essential that the country continues to succeed in assimilating its immigrants, because failure may result in future efforts to divide the country along ethnic lines similar to the situation in Canada, where French-speaking citizens of Quebec wished to disaffiliate from the rest of Canada. Or it may lead to devastating internal strife like that in Afghanistan, Sri Lanka, Angola, Burundi, and some other African countries – and a few American cities. The CIS study referred to above further concluded that the tide of immigrants, who are generally poorer, less well educated and more inclined to receive welfare, is having a profound, historic, and generally harmful effect on the country. Integrating them into American society constitutes a major problem. The idea suggests itself that now may be the time to drastically cut back on immigration of all kinds until the assimilation process is further along.

The government is currently trying to locate and keep track of aliens in this country who are either terrorists or potential terrorists. This is a difficult task. To assist in accomplishing this objective, the Immigration and Naturalization Service is developing a computerized tracking system which is scheduled to come on line in the year 2003. When it does come on line, it may not be particularly effective because it will have no data on foreigners who entered the United States for the past 15 or 20 years. This is because Congress back then rescinded a long-standing law that required foreigners to report their whereabouts to the Post Office annually.

Unlike trying to locate and keep tract of potential terrorists, the task of locating freeloading aliens is a simple task because they report regularly to receive their welfare or unemployment benefits. Their names and current addresses are known. All immigrants, legal and illegal, receiving any kind of welfare or unemployment should be deported as eaters forthwith to their country of origin. All that is lacking is the will to do it. Cracking down on alien welfare recipients will go far towards improving the producer/eater ratio and will save the United States and the various states in the United States billions of dollars.

B. Illegals.

Mexico is the largest source of immigrants into the United States today, both legal and illegal. In 1997, the Immigration and Naturalization Service estimated that there were 2.7 million Mexicans in the U.S. illegally. In year 2002, it is probably around three million.

Attempts to illegally cross the Mexican-U.S. border have been estimated at between 1.2 and 1.6 million a year, but a tighter job market in the U.S., improvements in the Mexican economy, and tougher border controls may reduce that number to below 1.2 million in 2002. Nobody knows how many different people these numbers represent because the same people are often arrested multiple times. A study by Mexico's National Population Council, a Ministry of the Interior agency, published a report in 2002 entitled "Migration: Mexico-United States", which concluded that the massive flow of legal and illegal Mexican immigrants into the United States is structural and permanent, cannot be stopped, and won't decrease dramatically even if the Mexican economy blooms. The Council also reported that illegal immigrants don't give up after a failed border crossing attempt. Seven in ten deportees intend to try a new crossing in the next seven days, and most try again within days or hours. They consider the "forced returns" as part of the difficulty of making the entry. The Immigration and Naturalization Service calculated in 1998 that 1.4 to 1.5 million illegal aliens are arrested by the U.S. Border Patrol trying to enter the U.S. illegally each year, but estimated that another 150,000 succeed in entering the country undetected. Others estimate that the total is much higher – 250,000 or even 400,000. The fact is that nobody really knows for sure.

The U.S. Code provides both criminal and civil penalties for illegal or attempted legal entry into the country, but the penalties are not commonly invoked against those illegally crossing the border from Mexico to the U.S. Polls have shown that Americans favored tighter controls on illegal immigration, even before the September 11, 2001 attacks on the World Trade Center and the Pentagon so they can be presumed to be even more in favor of tighter controls since September 11. This raises two questions:

The first is, should these penalties be invoked? According to a National Academy of Sciences report funded by the U.S. Commission on Immigration issued in 1997, immigrants add up to $10 billion to the U.S. economy each year, but immigrants may be costing some states and cities more than they add. It is undoubtedly true that the immigration of poor, low-skilled Mexican immigrants benefits certain industries such as the agriculture and restaurant industries by taking low-paying jobs. For example, according to the Department of Labor, there were 600,000 illegal immigrants working on U.S. farms in 1995, or 37 percent of the agricultural work force. At the same time, some of the jobs they take may be ones that low-skilled native workers would otherwise have taken. Thus, they compete with and adversely affect Mexican immigrants, blacks and unskilled whites who are already living here in the United States.

Beyond arguments that immigrants contribute to the economy, there are other arguments supporting the proposition that the present level of illegal immigration should be allowed to continue unabated. One is that immigration is necessary to maintain the population of the United States at its present level. Authorities contend that it takes 2.1 children per woman just to keep a society at zero growth. America's fertility rate has averaged about two children per woman in recent years, not enough to maintain the current level of population. Immigrant women have more than 2.1 children on average, which tends to lift the average for the country as a whole. However, this argument is a nonstarter since there is no showing that the country wants to or needs to either increase or even maintain its present population level.

The argument cannot be made because the world is surely overpopulated. The overpopulation is not as pronounced in the United States as it is in other countries such as Bangladesh, Indonesia, and some African countries where hundreds of thousands of people are starving or suffering from an insufficient supply of food, but the United States *is* nevertheless overpopulated to a degree, as evidenced by air and water pollution, in large cities like Los Angeles, California, and Birmingham, Alabama. It is people who pollute, and the best way to reduce pollution is to reduce population. At some point as population increases, the environment becomes unable to neutralize the waste produced by people.

A third argument is that political relationships between the United States, Mexico and other Latin American countries would be adversely affected if wet-backs illegally entering the United States were penalized. This is a valid argument, of course, and, to avoid or mitigate such an effect, the U.S. should – before starting to invoke penalties – conduct a thorough and far-reaching information campaign in Mexico and other Latin American countries, notifying the people there of its change in policy for enforcing the immigration laws. In this way, people in these countries who might be considering illegal immigration would be put on notice that the United States will no longer serve as the safety valve for their countries' excess populations and the probable consequences that would follow for the individual from an attempt at illegal immigration after a certain specified date.

There is another reason for curtailing illegal immigration besides reducing competition for jobs. Because the Mexican homeland is contiguous to the United States and because the overriding motive for Mexicans immigrating into this country is for economic reasons, they have very little motivation for integrating into the American society and culture. That would be at least part of the explanation for the fact that only 15 percent of the estimated seven million Mexican immigrants in 1997 had become U.S. citizens.

The second question is what kind of penalty (punishment) could the United States invoke? Community service and probation are out of the question on the face of it. The other two modes of punishment used in the United States today are fines and imprisonment. Fines are out of the question because these people have no money. If they had, they would not be trying to immigrate illegally. The United States could not afford and does not have the prison capacity to imprison 1.4 to 1.5 million people caught trying to illegally immigrate, so that also is out of the question. Another form of punishment is indicated, one of those described in Chapter 8. In this case, the punishment for the first offense would necessarily be corporal – flogging or caning. It is quick and cheap. No trial is necessary. These people are invaders. Before deportation and after flogging, they would receive notification of a more severe penalty for ever getting caught trying again to enter the country illegally. That punishment might be consignment to hard labor for a period of years building roads or working in mines in a remote region of northern Alaska. Second offenders would be easily identified by the scars they carry from the first offense and, again, consigned without trial as invaders. Those that facilitate illegal immigration (coyotes or snakes) should receive the more severe punishment the first time they are caught. Such enforcement would not only go a long way towards avoiding a further deterioration in the U.S. producer/eater ratio, but would also reduce by billions of dollars the cost of patrolling the U. S.-Mexican border.

Chapter 8. Prisoners.

A. Prisons.

One of the largest pools of eaters is found in the nation's prisons. A small minority of people in prisons is mentally deranged to one extent or another, or are genuinely wicked people, and must be separated from the general population because of the harm they are likely to do if released. Most of the people in prison are not really bad. Some are not adequately motivated to work, but the primary reason they are in prison is because they had no money and no marketable skills to use in earning money in a legal way. So, to get money, they committed illegal acts. Most of them didn't want to commit illegal acts because committing illegal acts is stressful and often dangerous – robbing a bank or dealing drugs, for example. Most of them would have preferred to do something legal to get money, but there was nothing they could do that anyone would pay them for. Some prisoners produce something in prison, but most don't. They are eaters.

There are nearly two million people currently in federal and state prisons and local jails according to a recent Department of Justice report. Thus, one of every 141 U.S. residents is behind bars. Prisons have revolving doors. Between one-third and one-half of the prison population is released every year, and about two-thirds of those released are rearrested and reimprisoned, many times while they are still on parole. In addition to inmates of federal and state prisons and local jails, about 105,000 others are held in various facilities like territorial prisons, immigration facilities, and Native American jails. At an estimated annual cost of $25,000 for the custodial cost of each of the 2 million prisoners, the U.S. is spending $50 billion a year, which amounts to about $340 for each of the 147 million people in the United States between the ages of 25 and 64. (This is the age bracket of the nation's producers, although not all of them are producers by any means.) A person age 25 will pay $13,600, during the 40 years on average he will be productive, to support prisoners. There are another 3.9 million Americans on probation or parole, adding further to the costs of the nation's penal system.

Certainly, imprisonment is the most expensive known form of punishment. The prisoner must be fed, clothed, housed in an expensive structure, provided with medical and dental care, and guarded around the clock. His family also may have to be supported by society while he is in prison. Taxpayers and legislators alike are concerned about the rising cost of maintaining growing prison populations. One answer to the problem has been for governments to privatize prisons, a program that has been moderately successful in cutting costs, but which is subject to criticism because contractors, in their zeal for profits, may not take adequate care of the prisoners. Judges have been resorting to alternative forms of punishment such as sentences to probation, home detention and community service. Parole boards in some areas have become more lenient, often out of necessity as the prison populations exceed the capacities of existing prisons. With all of this, the penal system is still very costly.

People are disturbed by the rising incidence of crime and they, along with prosecutors, are demanding stronger deterrents -- stiffer (longer) sentences. More criminals plus longer sentences mean more increases in the prison populations, which will continue to overtax the capacities of these institutions. More and bigger prisons are not the answer. Taxpayers do not want to and cannot afford to pay for them, and imprisonment as a form of punishment is not having the desired effect.

Punishment is definitely one effect of imprisonment, and an effect much desired by most victims of crimes. Depriving an individual of his freedom, keeping him from friends and family for a period of years is, indeed, a most severe form of punishment.

When a prisoner is finally released, he may find that his former girlfriend has married another. His wife (if he had one) has divorced him and remarried. His children have grown and don't really know him anymore, and his former friends have died or moved away. He still suffers from the lack of marketable skills which is what probably put him behind bars in the first place and which is likely to cause him to wind up there again. He is worse off than before he went to prison because, after his release, he has a prison record, which makes it doubly hard to find legal employment. Prison terms of years ruin lives absolutely.

There is an ongoing debate about whether imprisonment deters crime. It should but often does not for several reasons: First, the prospective criminal can see the immediate benefits of his crime if successful. The punishment is uncertain and more difficult to visualize. Second, even if he is successful in visualizing imprisonment as the consequence of his crime, he may not find it all that distasteful compared to his present circumstances. As one prisoner said to a newspaper reporter, "You get a hot [shower] and a cot [bed] and get to see all of your friends." What good is the freedom to travel around, go to the store or a movie, if one has no money to do these things, the usual predicament of most potential criminals? Third, he may overestimate his capabilities for avoiding detection of his crime and so go ahead with it, whereas he might not if he were more realistic.

Prisons were originally called penitentiaries because they were places of detention where offenders against the law were sent for short periods of time to do penance for their evil ways and be restored to society as useful citizens. Long sentences handed down by judges today have the undesirable effect of causing attitudes of hostility and bitterness towards society that are just the opposite of the penitent attitudes incarceration was originally intended to produce, and there is no evidence that prisoners today do much in the way of penitence. The more enlightened individuals among us like to think of imprisonment as "behavioral correction" and like to use such politically correct terms as "correction centers" or "correctional institutions" to describe warehouses for criminals. But, as with penitence, there is very little correction done in penal institutions today and probably never was much.

Occasionally, we hear about a prisoner who learned a legitimate trade during the term of his incarceration, which he was able to put to good use for earning an honest living after he was released. When one considers that these prisoners, as children, had the opportunity for 12 years of free publicly-financed education which did not take, it is unlikely that the most of them are going to learn anything legally useful in prison. To the contrary, all too often, other skills are learned from contacts with hardened criminals that foster a continued life of crime after release.

Common sense tells us the underlying causes for crime are money and passion. Underlying both of these causes is usually sex. We are talking about the motivations of men here, because about 93 percent of the population of prisons and jails are men, and only 7 percent women. A man's desire is often to acquire sufficient money to attract a desirable woman who is willing to have regular, natural sex with him. It was Aristotle Onassis who said, "Money is nothing to men without women."

Women desire men who, among other things, have enough money and income to support a family. If a man is not able to earn enough money to support a family in a legal way and have access to regular, natural sex, he may turn to some illegal way for acquiring money. There are, of course, instances in which sex is not involved as a motivator for illegal activities. For example, men may be striving to make a great deal of money because making money is a game for them. He who dies with the most wins. To win, men engaged in this game may resort to less than ethical practices. Andrew S. Fastow of the Enron Corporation and Scott D. Sullivan of Worldcom might fall into this category. Sex also is involved directly in many – probably most – violent crimes of passion. Hence, the motto of police investigating such crimes: *cherchez la femme,* or look for the woman.

B. Reducing Prison Populations.

There are three ways to reduce the number of people in prisons: The first and best way is to reduce the number of people who have committed a crime, and that can only be done by reducing the number of men who reach adulthood without skills that they can use to earn a decent living for themselves and a family. This takes time and has to be started early in a child's life. The only way to do that is to allow only heterosexual, married couples to have or to adopt children, couples who want them, are willing to motivate them to learn, and are financially positioned to support them.

The second way is by providing more employment opportunities for those who come on the labor market without marketable skills. Changes need to be made so that they can get a job, earn a living -- at least for themselves – in a legal way, and lead reasonably happy lives. There are two ways of providing such employment: The first – speaking heresy at a time when there is a clamor to increase the minimum wage – is by repealing the minimum wage law, which would result in the creation of more low-paying jobs for which released prisoners, who are usually unskilled, could qualify.

Up until, perhaps, ten years after World War II, a young man with a strong, healthy body and little in the way of skills could earn a decent living and support a family. That has changed. Right after WWII, the United States had about the only large-scale manufacturing capability in the world. If a person bought a shirt or a sewing machine, it would have been one made in the United States. This was because the war decimated the manufacturing capabilities of European and Asian countries, but as they recovered – actually aided by the United States – their industries began to compete with U.S. industries. Lower wages and more modern machinery gave them an edge, and free trade gave them access to foreign markets, including those in the U.S.

Almost everyone is aware that the minimum wage (now $5.15 per hour) is a politically-determined amount legislated by the federal government and intended to raise wages of workers (of companies employing more than a certain number of employees) above the poverty level, which is arbitrarily determined by the federal government to be about $14,000 a year for a single parent (read mother) with two children. The market has nothing to do with determining either the minimum wage or the poverty level.

Employers affected by the minimum wage law react in various ways. If they are in a position where they can raise their prices, they may do so. McDonald's raises the price of Big Macs when the minimum wage is increased. If companies do raise prices, it means a hidden tax on customers buying their products. If companies are not in a position to raise prices, earnings are lower, stock prices are reduced, and stockholders suffer a loss. If it is a manufacturing plant that uses unskilled labor to perform repetitive-type production line tasks, the affected company may simply move it offshore to a country where cheaper, unskilled labor is available. Textile plants are a prime example of an entire industry that has moved offshore already. If it is a service industry, it may move certain parts of the operation offshore. Clerical and statistical operations of insurance companies and stock brokerages are prime examples of service industries that have moved parts of their operations offshore. In extreme cases – and particularly with smaller businesses – they may simply have to go out of business, causing a direct loss to the job market.

If manufacturing plants or operations cannot be moved offshore, companies may increase the use of technology and equipment to reduce the number of their employees. For example, if a person wants a ditch or other excavation dug today, he hires a contractor who comes with a backhoe and a semi-skilled operator to dig it. Both are expensive. If laborers could be hired at the market value of their services to do the digging manually with pick and shovel, contractors would often find that many jobs could be done more economically using cheap labor, rather than purchasing or leasing expensive machines and paying semi-skilled operators. As it is, unskilled manual labor at minimum wage is many times too expensive to compete with machines.

Similarly, if seamen could be hired at market value wages, many released prisoners could find unskilled work in the maritime service, and the United States merchant marine could be expanded and manned with American sailors. In all of these cases, jobs requiring little or no skills either have already been or will be lost in the future to those having little or no skill.

American environmentalists need to forget about Alaska as a pristine wilderness for preservation and begin thinking of it as a new frontier ready for development, albeit with due regard for the environment. The United States needs Alaska's resources. The U.S. should negotiate with Canada for an easement across western Canada east of the Rocky Mountains for construction of a railroad connecting the "lower 48," Alaska, and western Canada. Roads and railroads are needed within Alaska to begin development of the state's natural resources. These roads and railroads could be built entirely by the manual labor of prisoners.

The second way of providing more employment opportunities for not only released prisoners but unskilled and low skilled individuals generally is to empower the army to recruit and use labor brigades for public projects in the lower 48 much in the way that the Civilian Conservation Corps did during the Depression of the 1930s. Almost all of the excellent construction work the CCC did was done with manual labor, hand tools and explosives. Most of the work did not require skills. These brigades should be self-sufficient and, to become so, every prisoner in the brigade would have to learn a trade and practice it. The brigades would have their own prisoner-teachers, librarians, barbers, cooks, bakers, plumbers, carpenters, mechanics, managers, storekeepers, electricians, bricklayers, and other trades. There are many worthwhile projects that could be undertaken.

Individuals employed at market rates without benefit of minimum wage laws, those employed in developing Alaska, and those employed in army labor brigades would be able to afford only boarding house living accommodations. They would not be able to afford a wife and family. To be content at such low-level wages and in such living conditions, they would have to be provided with access to regular, natural sex -- usually by Friendship Houses.

C. Alternative Punishments.

The third way to reduce the population of prisons is to provide forms of punishment as alternatives to imprisonment and offer some of those already inside prisons alternative forms of punishment. There are seven forms of punishment meted out to criminals in the United States these days: fines, expropriation of property, imprisonment, probation, community service, home detention and – in relatively rare cases and at enormous expense to society for appeals – capital punishment. There are three others acceptable to western civilization: placarding, corporal punishment, and transportation. Two of these – corporal punishment and transportation – are not used at all.

Placarding criminals is a mild form of punishment for those found guilty of lesser offenses, such as spitting on the sidewalk (spitter) or those found guilty of mild spousal battery (wife beater). Punishment would be requiring them to walk about in a public place for a few days wearing a sandwich board announcing to the world the offense they had committed, Taxing authorities today use a device similar in purpose by publishing the names of delinquent taxpayers in local newspapers.

Why aren't corporal punishment and transportation used? One reason is that they are cheap, and legislators in this country seem to have an aversion towards anything that is inexpensive. Probably the biggest reason is that people consider such punishments to be cruel and unusual, inhumane, barbaric or uncivilized, but what could be more barbaric and uncivilized than locking a person up in a concrete fortress for a span of years away from society, family, and friends? For the most part, legislators -- like the rest of us – simply get into a mental rut and don't think about alternatives.

In selecting punishments, it behooves society to select not only those which are appropriate to the crime but also those which will have the greatest deterrent effect. Consideration must be given to what it is that people fear most. Is it death? Pain? Public humiliation? Isolation? Deprivation of property?

Corporal punishment, particularly if administered in the village square or city plaza, can combine pain with public humiliation. These are two of the greatest fears of man, and the threat of them is a most powerful deterrent. Consider the plight of the person who has only to speak before an audience. His mouth becomes dry as dust, and his knees shake – all from fear of humiliating himself. Some people fear being humiliated more than death. Corporal punishment can take many forms. Parents – some would say unenlightened parents – spank their children on occasion. In Singapore, criminals are flayed across the buttocks with a rattan. The British once flogged criminals across the back with a cat-of-nine-tails to the same effect. If this is not overdone, the pain and mortification are transitory, and the person punished can return to his job and to society in a couple of weeks duly chastened.

Corporal punishment does not have to be violent. Early colonists in this country used the stocks. Standing or sitting in the stocks located in a public place for several days must have been exceedingly uncomfortable and most humiliating. Early colonists had to use such punishments; they could not afford much in the way of jails even if they wished to incarcerate.

Transportation to a remote and distant place, never to return, has been widely used in Western civilization. The British colonized a state or two in this country and the countries of Australia and New Zealand by transporting criminals. The USSR initially populated Siberia by transporting criminals and political dissidents. It is an acceptable form of punishment. Transporting criminals is probably the only way that many remote regions in Alaska will ever be populated and the great mineral wealth of that state exploited. Transportation effectively insulates the parent society forever from the hardened criminal and any more of his criminal acts. Fear of transportation never to return may be a strong deterrent to crime in much the same way as the fear of imprisonment may deter. However, unlike prison inmates, transportees would have a chance to make a new life for themselves in a new and, albeit, rugged environment in much the same way as did British criminals who were transported to the state of Georgia and to Australia. The costs of maintaining prisoners in remote regions of Alaska would be minimal because the very remoteness would obviate the need for expensive prison structures and many guards.

Chapter 9. Welfare Recipients.

A. Medicare "B."

Medicare "B" is simply medical insurance. It is not welfare. The policyholder agrees to pay a monthly premium (usually by a deduction from his monthly Social Security income), and the government agrees to pay certain of his medical expenses. The policyholder is free to terminate the policy at any time he wishes, and the government is also free to do so. Political considerations aside, the government should do so and get out of the insurance business.

B. Medicaid.

Medicaid is another story. Here, there is no consideration, and Medicaid is simply a *nudum pactum* or naked promise by which the government does something for the indigent. Thus, Medicaid is not legally enforceable, and the government could legally terminate the program if it wished to do so at any time. Politically, of course, it would be difficult. It is a program in two parts: on the one hand, it benefits principally poor mothers and their children by providing them with medical care and, on the other hand, it benefits indigent old people by providing them with assisted living and nursing home and other medical and warehousing care. Therefore, Medicaid needs to be considered in two parts: The first part needs to be retained and enlarged because it provides for children in the pipeline who have prospects of becoming our future producers. With proper medical care, the nation can expect a higher proportion of producers emerging from the pipeline than it otherwise could. The opposite is true for the part of Medicaid that provides for the care and feeding of indigent old people. Termination of this part of Medicaid would do more

163

than anything else to quickly improve the producer-eater ratio because the indigent elderly would no longer be able to afford the drugs, medical care, and surgical procedures needed to keep them alive. Options for aged Medicaid recipients are discussed in Chapter 11.

C. Supplemental Security Income.

This program, established by the 1972 Social Security Act amendments, provided income for 6.5 million needy, aged, blind and disabled persons in the year 2003 at a cost of $33 billion. This also is a *nudum pactum* which the government can legally terminate with the same beneficial effects on the producer/eater ratio as terminating the part of Medicaid that provides for the elderly. Options of such people are also discussed in Chapter 11, along with those of aged Medicaid recipients.

D. Welfare for Domestic Corporations, Industries and Foreign Countries.

Subsidies for domestic corporations, industries, and foreign countries are probably the second most expensive type of welfare recipients. Because of the many forms such welfare takes, it is impossible to quantify it.

E. Welfare for the Poor.

Welfare, as we commonly think of it in all of its many forms (food stamps, subsidized housing, free breakfasts and lunches in schools, aid with utility payments, tax breaks, to name a few) needs to be continued to the extent that it benefits children and for the same reason that part of Medicaid should be continued. With success in reducing the number of potential eaters in the pipeline, the need for Medicaid and welfare for children should diminish over time, and both programs could eventually be curtailed or perhaps even terminated. Actually, much more needs to be done for poor children than society presently does. In many cases, these children would be benefitted by providing a means for allowing them to be removed from their home environment and placed in excellent boarding schools.

F. Welfare for Incumbent Politicians (Pork).

Usually, all forms of welfare can also be appropriately classified as pork welfare. Pork, the most egregious form of welfare, is a benefit to incumbent legislators in their quests to be reelected. Pork is the worst kind of corruption, but our wily legislators have legalized it. It is paid – not directly to incumbent legislators themselves – but to benefit those individuals, companies, and industries that contribute to their reelection campaigns. Benefits to campaign contributors come in the form of orders for defense materiel (that the Department of Defense doesn't want), protective tariffs, price supports and the like. Pork also pays for projects of various sorts that are of uncertain benefit to the nation as a whole, but which are intended to benefit the legislator's own constituents. They are in the form of bridges and roads of little use, unneeded veterans' hospitals, minimum wage legislation, et cetera. The list goes on. Almost every budget bill is loaded with such pork of little or no benefit to anyone except the legislator, his campaign contributors, and his own constituents. In this way, a significant portion of the nation's wealth is redistributed for at least the secondary and often primary purpose of reelecting legislators. Because the pork takes so many forms, exactly how much it amounts to is hard to tell. At election time, legislators like to boast of the amount of pork they have brought to their state or district. With advantages like this that they have, it is nearly impossible to unseat a sitting legislator unless he has been found to have committed one or more egregiously immoral acts. How to avoid this kind of welfare is discussed in Part III.

Chapter 10. Life, Death and Killing.

Before undertaking a discussion of those ways of improving the producer/eater ratio, which involve the harsh measures of abortion, feticide, suicide, assisted suicide, and euthanasia, it is important to try to reach an understanding and, hopefully, some form of consensus on life, death, and killing.

A. Life, What Is It?

Nobody, including religionists, really knows what life is. That's a fact, but people feel a need to know about matters affecting their lives and, when they cannot have facts, they are amenable to myths and theories – anything that sounds reasonably plausible. Religions theorize that life (spirit, soul) is a God-given immaterial and supernatural essence that animates organic creatures.

I submit that life is a primary form of energy along with gravity, magnetism, nuclear (including solar) and chemical energy. We see these primary energies all around us in various forms. Tides, falling and flowing water, and the weights that power most grandfather clocks are common manifestations of gravitational energy. We are all familiar with the attraction exerted by magnetism on iron and steel. The directional compass is powered by magnetism. Static electricity exerts a magnetic force on some organic substances. Sunshine is the most common manifestation of nuclear energy. We see chemical energy all around us in various forms but the most common is combustion (rapid oxidation).
Science has a store of knowledge about the five forms of primary energy in varying degrees. Most is probably known about chemical energy, followed by nuclear energy. Much research is devoted to learning more about nuclear energy, particularly nuclear fusion which, unlike nuclear fission, has the potential of producing derivative forms of energy without contaminating the

environment. The discovery that the interruption of a magnetic field would produce a flow of electrons in a wire (electricity) was very likely a fortunate happenstance. Probably least is known about gravitational energy. For example, are there gravitational fields that could be interrupted like magnetic fields to produce a more usable derivative form of energy? Neither is much known about life energy, although a great deal of effort is currently being devoted to achieving a greater understanding of it.

From the primary forms of energy come secondary forms. The sun (solar) shines on green plants which, by the process of photosynthesis (chemical), produces (among other things) food. Arguably, photosynthesis is the most useful form of energy because it nourishes all living organisms.Cellulose, produced by photosynthesis, when burned (chemical) produces steam which turns a generator (motion) which breaks a magnetic field (magnetic) to produce electricity, probably our third most useful form of energy. Gravity (falling water), and nuclear forms of energy are used in the same way to produce electricity, which can be transported and used to produce motion, heat and light as tertiary forms of energy.

There are three forms of life's secondary energy. The most common manifestation of life energy in animals is movement or the ability to move. Life energy, when infused into an organism (a hydrocarbon), produces small amounts of electricity (chemical), which actuates tissue, causing it to elongate and contract, producing motion. It also produces what is arguably the second most useful of all forms of secondary energy – thought. Life energy (in the form of thought and motion) is also combined with other primary forms of energy to produce derivative secondary and tertiary forms of energy. Emotions, a third form, which are characterized by pleasure or pain, by attraction or repulsion and the like, are partly mental and partly physical responses to external stimuli. These are very powerful determiners of human behavior.

It is now widely accepted scientifically that energy, like matter, can be neither created nor destroyed. If one accepts this theory and that life is a primary form of energy, then the facts that apply to all forms of energy apply to life. It can be converted to matter, as when plants convert sunlight into tissue (matter) by photosynthesis. Alternatively, mass can be converted to motion and to thought (energy) as when food is eaten and digested by a living creature (chemical and electrical). Its form can be changed but that's all. Thus, after life energy has departed an organism, the life energy vested in the organism before death still exists. But *where* it exists is a mystery.

One might deduce from the life cycles of insects that humans also would be recreated eventually in human form rather than as, for example, a tree or an elephant. Insects go through their life cycles without becoming anything other than what they were. Would this be a direct conversion? That is, when someone dies, is another human being somewhere on the face of the earth conceived to receive the spirit? Or is there a life energy reservoir to which spirits departing the body go for a time and are only later consigned to another body. Absent such a reservoir, it would be difficult to explain how the tremendous increase in the population of humans on earth could have taken place over the past 100 years unless, of course, the spirit is consigned immediately to a human body in another dimension, a dimension which we cannot detect with our five senses.

Many people feel that new life is created when an egg is fertilized by a sperm cell, but that is not true, because both the egg and the sperm were alive before the fertilization took place. Fertilization creates a separate living organism – not new life. All living organisms (that is, all creatures imbued with life energy) have the ability to reproduce. They have the ability to produce cells that can reproduce similar cells and also the ability to produce cells that have the potential for reproducing a whole new organism of the same kind. For example, skin cells in a human being, cells which are living, can reproduce themselves so that all the while some skin cells are dying, new ones are reproduced to take their places. An egg cell, on the other hand, once fertilized with sperm, has the ability to reproduce, not just another egg, but a whole new organism. Both the egg and the sperm are alive prior to their interaction, but it is only their union that enables the two cells to become a whole new organism. Exactly what transpires to cause this effect is a mystery.

There may be two states of life energy — vested and unvested. All vested life is the same, appearing to be different only because of the difference in appearance of the organism in which it is vested. It animates all living creatures alike, whether macro- or microscopic, plant or animal. The life vested in a mosquito or a cabbage is the same as that vested in a human being. The organism varies, but not the energy. Grinding up kernels of wheat takes the same life energy from an organism as slaughtering a steer. Vested life is everywhere. There is some vested life in the most arid deserts and in the blackest depths of the oceans and the coldest regions of Antarctica. Life is in the air we breathe, the water we drink, the food we eat, and our bodies are full of life other than our own (bacteria, fungi, spores, and viruses).

As well as the vested life apparent to us, there may be vested life all around us in an entirely different dimension that we, as adults, are unable to detect. Almost universally very young children detect at one time or another, an alien presence in their bedroom. They call their parent. The parent "knows" that there is no alien presence in the room but, to reassure the child, the parent turns on the light, looks under the bed, and opens the closet, demonstrating to the child that there is nothing there. Reassured, the child goes to sleep. As the child grows older, he gradually loses the ability to detect such life. Long before he has grown to adulthood, he has lost it entirely. Did the child really detect a presence that the parent could not?

Unvested life may be all around us as well in the same way that gravity is everywhere. If one accepts this idea, then the reservoir of unvested life energy must be what we call God, and every living creature has a tiny spark of the same God vested in him, her, or it. It may be that some individuals are able somehow to tap into that vast reservoir of unvested energy to accomplish unbelievable deeds. Jesus Christ – if, indeed, he did perform even a few of the marvelous acts reported in the Bible – may have done so by being in touch with this gigantic unvested reservoir of energy that may fill the universe. In touch with God, if you will. Perhaps, he learned somehow to do this during the 40 days he roamed in the desert? Outstanding decision-makers and performers of all kinds *feel* more than they actually *think*. As Robert Redford once said about acting: "It's something you don't want to think too much about."

All civilizations have had religion of some kind. Generally, these religions presuppose an all-powerful entity that controls what happens to us at death, may control our lives in this world and, indeed, may control the entire universe and everything in it. It cannot hurt to try to curry favor with such an entity through worship. Humankind has a need to worship. The need probably stems from the fact that we realize that someday we will die, and we do not know for sure what will happen to us when we do. Some civilizations have worshiped volcanoes. Others worshiped various animals. The Aztecs worshiped the sun which is not a bad idea since the continuation of all life is dependent upon the sun. Still others worshiped inanimate objects or icons. Worship manifests itself in the form of sacrifice, penance and praise.

God is life and life is God, but it is very difficult for humans to worship life as a form of energy because neither life energy nor any other primary energy can be seen, heard, smelled,

171

felt, tasted, or touched. Could you, for example worship gravity? Or magnetism? Not likely. So, we find it convenient to substitute some object or creature that we can be aware of with our five senses. For example, the Bible says that God made Jesus in his own image. Ergo, since Jesus looked like a man, God must also look like a man. God does not look like a man, of course, because God is life, and life does not look like anything. A man is easily visualized.

B. Death, What Is It?

Medically, death is the permanent cessation of all vital functions of an organism. It is the departure of the life energy from the organism. If the organism breathed before death, it does not breathe afterwards. It does not move. It is no longer able to ward off the assaults of ever-present bacteria, and the tissues of the organism begin to rot. The questions that people want answered are not "What is it?" but rather what happens to us upon death? Where does one's spirit or life go? What does it feel like and more specifically, does it hurt? Nobody has ever returned from the dead to tell us specifically and authoritatively the answers to these questions but, short of that, we do have rather specific information.

There is another way to look at the end of life. The dictionary says that death is the end of life, but the end of life may come long before death. It can end without death. How can one tell when life is ended, if not at death? Think of a newborn baby. All it can do at first is breathe, defecate, urinate, suckle, and cry. Everything else has to be done for it. Parents must feed, clothe, shelter, bathe, dress, and generally provide all of the care for infants. Later, it learns to smile, to move its eyes, arms, fingers, and legs. It recognizes its mother's face. It learns to eat with a spoon, to roll over by itself, and to crawl on all fours. By

172

and by, it learns to walk upright, to talk, to dress itself, and to tie its shoe laces. As the child grows older, it becomes self-sufficient except for providing its food, clothing, shelter, and education. Eventually, the child becomes an adult and is fully self-sufficient. Later, the adult marries, has children and then provides, not only for himself, but also for his children, his spouse and, perhaps, for one or more of his or his spouse's parents. Adults are able to go on for years this way caring for themselves, their children and others and, sometimes, putting aside money for their own use when they grow old and are unable to work anymore.

Time passes. The adult's children leave home and become self-sufficient. The aged parents die. The adult continues to age and, if death does not intervene, he eventually becomes infirm in one or more ways. When the adult becomes so infirm that he can no longer take care of himself (let alone anybody else) and when the likelihood is that he never again will be able to, his life is actually over at that point. He has passed through the cycle from infant, to adult, to infirm. His life is over although his heart has not stopped beating. He is then a burden on society. Instead of being part of the solution, he has become part of the problem. Nursing homes are full of people in this condition, people who would be clinically dead were it not for the marvels of the medical arts and the care of the nursing home attendants.

That is the most common way to know when life is over, except, of course, for a person's actual death. Another way is when a person is afflicted with intense, unrelenting pain (or any other condition such as continual nausea) that takes the joy out of living, and it appears that the condition will be permanent. Homeless people living on the streets, eating out of dumpsters, sleeping under bridges or in doorways with no hope of improving their situation are also an example of people at the end of their lives, although not yet clinically dead. Some of them are people who worked and provided for themselves (and perhaps others) at one time but failed to provide for themselves in their in their declining years. Poor nutrition, exposure, and lack of medical care often mercifully shorten the period of living death for the homeless.

We all fall asleep every night (with the exception of a few people) without fear of doing so. We welcome sleep. That is because we have fallen asleep over and over again, and believe with considerable assurance that the next morning we will wake up. Everyone will agree that the sleep state is not the same as the awake state. Neither is it the same as the death state, but there are similarities between the sleep state and the death state. Do we make a temporary visit to the other side of the curtain when we sleep, keeping one foot safely in this life? Are some of our dreams representations of experiences we have had, will have or could have on the other side of the curtain? As with death, nobody really knows what sleep is or what dreams are.

The Bible (Corinthians) says, "O death, where is thy sting? Actually, available evidence indicates that there is no sting; it feels pretty good. How can one know this since none of us have ever died and come back? We know because death is a bodily function (albeit a one-time function for each of us) just like any other bodily function including eating, drinking water, breathing, urinating, defecating, vomiting, or having an orgasm. First, one feels pain or discomfort leading up to the function. Then, one experiences considerable pleasure from the function as it is being performed and, afterwards, one feels very good. Take for example, thirst and drinking water. Most of us today never really become thirsty because water is always handy, but, if you can remember having been really thirsty, you know how uncomfortable that feeling is. Then, the sheer pleasure of a cool drink of water as you quench your thirst. And afterwards, one feels very good. Why should death be any different than the other bodily functions?

Bolstering this conclusion are the accounts of people who have had near-death experiences which indicate that the journey across the bar is quite pleasant. Although many people give little credence to descriptions of the near-death experiences of others, these accounts should not be entirely discounted because there are so many of them, and most of them have certain similarities. Generally, these people say that they saw a very bright light as they died. Some have reported seeing people there, sometimes deceased relatives. Others have reported that they saw their own corpse and the activity going on around it. All of these people felt good as they died or seemed to die. Many felt so good that they did not really want to return to this world, but some responsibility, such as their need to care for small children, overcame their desire not to return, and they did.

There is also anecdotal evidence that a person's physical pain slips away as one dies. For example, an article appeared in the *Reader's Digest* several years ago about a family who ran a small mom and pop grocery store in the Bronx. The father had been shot in the shoulder years ago during an earlier robbery, and that shoulder hurt him constantly ever after. During a later robbery, he was shot again – this time fatally. As he lay dying in his son's arms, he exclaimed in wonderment, "My shoulder doesn't hurt me anymore."

Release from all pain, discomfort, obligations, and worry comes with death. Death can be looked upon as a gift bestowed upon us at birth, a gift which is the ultimate solution to any and all problems or troubles we may ever have, but it can be used only once. Indeed, it must be used once. In summary, death is not the fearsome prospect that some would have us believe it to be. Life prepares people for death. As one advances in age, friends and relatives die, the senses fade, life begins to lose its zest, pain and discomfort increase to a point where one may eventually regard death as a release from life's bondage.

The hereafter is where life (the soul) goes after death. Where is that? Nobody – including religionists – really knows where life goes when it departs the body of a living creature, but the religions have theories which most people believe because they want to believe. They want to believe because they are afraid of the unknown when they die. In the Christian religion, the theory is that, if a person leads a good, honest, upright life, that person will rise up to heaven when he dies, become an angel with wings and fly around paradise forever in the presence of God. If not, the person will descend into hell where he will burn forever in an atmosphere of brimstone and be prodded with pitchforks by agents of the devil with horns and pointy tails. Many people don't really believe these things but go along anyway because it can do no harm and (who knows) might do some good. Other religions have similar theories.

Although some of these theories are a bit fanciful, they are not to be deprecated because the benefits to society from religions promulgating such theories are immeasurable. Out of them, morals ensue. Morals are the rules – inspired most of the time by religions – that we are taught to *want* to follow so that we will behave in a way that is beneficial to society. Laws are rules enacted by government that cause us to be punished if we do not behave in a way beneficial to society. Both are necessary to society but, of the two, morals are undoubtedly the more necessary.

Beneficial as these theories may be, there is a different theory about what happens to our souls when we die. That different theory is that when we die, our life goes back to the exact same place or dimension from whence it came before we were born. Although people are very much interested in what happens to them when they die, we are not particularly interested in where we came from when we were born because that is an event that is already behind us. However, people should be interested because, if this theory is correct, where we came from is probably the best clue to what really happens to us when we die.

Adults cannot detect life on the other side of the curtain with our five senses, although it may very well be detectable. Babies may bring with them from the other side of the curtain considerable memory of what it is like there but, unfortunately by the time they are able to communicate with us, they have forgotten it in the same way that they lose their ability to detect presences under the bed. Actually, it is quite possible that there really is a presence in the child's bedroom which he can detect with senses he was born with, senses carried over from the environment he came from before he was born, but senses he will lose as he grows older. The parent has long ago lost these senses and can detect nothing in the bedroom. Is it possible that someday science will discover a means by which adults can detect life on the other side of the curtain? No? Well, who would have thought a hundred years ago that I could sit in my living room in Alexandria, Virginia today and view in real time, living color and surround sound the Yankees playing a baseball game in New York City?

Without such means, we may still know a lot about the environment that life (soul) enters when it leaves worldly bodies. Consider, first, that almost everything in the universe proceeds in cycles. Think of it this way: there are two seasons, summer and winter. We pass from one to the other over and over again as the earth revolves around the sun. Spring and fall are merely transitional periods from one season to the other that we have added as a convenience to identify the in-between periods. As the earth rotates on its axis, we experience day and night. Morning and evening are merely transitional periods like spring and fall. The moon cycles around the earth.

Is it unreasonable to conclude that we cycle in the same way between life in this world and death in the hereafter, wherever or whatever that may be? If one accepts that lives cycle, then is it not logical to assume that lives return to the same environment they came from when they entered this world at birth? If one accepts the concept of lives cycling, then is it not also reasonable to conclude that conditions in the environment beyond death would be similar to conditions for lives upon coming into this world at birth? Admittedly, there is no hard evidence to support this theory, but it seems to be logical when considered in light of what we know about the cyclical nature of the universe we live in.

If one accepts these conclusions, then the next step is to consider what conditions we find at birth. We need air constantly. We are born into a sea of it. Unless we become trapped under water, we can hardly get into a situation where we cannot readily get air. Next most frequently, we need water. Water is nearly everywhere, covering two-thirds of the earth's surface. True, most of it is salty. Although marine plants and animals can live in salty water, humans and other land animals and plants cannot survive on salty water. We need fresh water, but our parents tend to live in areas where there is enough fresh water. Next, we need food. For those newly born, mothers have a special food produced in their breasts – milk. Later when the baby needs solid food, it can be found in the form of plants everywhere that there is fresh, liquid water. Where there are plants, there are animals that can be slaughtered for solid food. Most important of all, the new entrant into this world is blessed with two parents programmed to look to its every need for food, water, shelter, clothing, education, and love. Not such a bad environment to be born into. Is it not reasonable to conclude that conditions in the hereafter are similarly well designed and appointed for the well-being of our lives when they arrive there?

C. Killing.

The dictionary says that killing is the depriving of life or causing death. One of the Ten Commandments (the sixth) says, "Thou shalt not kill." Does that mean that it is a sin (immoral) to kill anything? Certainly not. Some animals are nourished by eating plants, killing them in the process, in whole or in part. Other animals feed on these animals, killing them in the process. Human beings feed on both. Thus, some living organisms must die in order that others may live, and, usually, that means they must be killed. For there to be life, there must be death, because all living creatures have to eat other plants and animals that have lived. Killing is necessary for human beings to live. Most human beings do not actually do the killing. They pay others to do the killing for them, but there can be no life without death. Death is necessary for life.

Many people have singularly odd and inconsistent views about killing animals. Recall the ruckus that took place on the sea ice in the far North a few years ago when a group of Americans were involved in protesting the bludgeoning of baby Harp seals to death and harvesting them for their white fur. Others here in the United States, to protest the killing of fur-bearing animals, threw paint on women wearing fur coats. These same people wear leather shoes and belts made from the hides of animals, and relish dinners of roasted lamb without experiencing any conflict with their morals. People also exhibit inconsistencies regarding the kinds of meat they will eat. Christian people in this country will eat cows, pigs, sheep, turkeys and chickens but will not eat horses, rats, cats, or dogs. Muslims and Jews will not eat pig meat. Hindus will not eat cow meat. As a further inconsistency, if most people had to kill the animal they were to eat, they would not be able to eat the meat. Somebody else has to do the killing. Then they can eat the meat.

Specifically then, what do the words, "Thou shalt not kill" mean? Generally speaking, people may kill any plant or animal that they own without committing sin or violating the law. Livestock and poultry are slaughtered in large numbers daily. All kinds of plants are picked, mowed down, and packed off for food daily as well. However, killing a plant or animal owned by another is almost always illegal and immoral, not because the killing takes the life of the plant or animal but, because the killing violates the owner's property rights or infringes upon the rights of the state to collect revenue (license fees) or to protect the environment (endangered species). Unnecessary, wanton, or sadistic killing of any living organism is a sin and may also be illegal. But the words of the Ten Commandments necessarily allude to the killing of a human being.

Although the killing of humans (homicide) is usually held to be immoral and illegal, there are exceptions. Killing in self-defense, in defense of a family member, or in defense of a person's home is usually considered to be excusable and not immoral or illegal. Accidental killing of a human, if not done through gross negligence, is usually not punishable under law. Killing combatants from another country with which the killer's own country is at war is both legal and encouraged. Killing of felons by officials of the State is justifiable and not immoral or illegal when directed by a court of proper jurisdiction. Society has set the rules for killing to suit its own purposes.

Why is it usually both illegal and immoral to kill human beings when it is not illegal and immoral to kill plants and other animals that are the property of the killer or his organization? The life that is taken is the same; it is simply the organism that is different. The answer is that if one kills an oak tree, a fish, a fly or a rabbit, he may do so without fear of retaliation, but if one kills another person, the situation is entirely different. It is different because the victim has kin and, if society does nothing, the kin of the victim will seek revenge. Feuding will break out, and society will begin to break down. To prevent such developments, society makes moral and legal rules against killing other humans, sets up a judicial system for determining guilt, and imposes penalties. When the families of victims feel that justice has been done, peace is restored without feuding.

Chapter 11. Reducing the Number of Eaters.

A. Abortions.

Under the statutory law in effect in most states up until the famous U.S. Supreme Court case of *Roe v. Wade (1973)*, abortion, except when necessary to preserve the pregnant woman's life, was a criminal offense. These laws were of a relatively recent vintage having derived from statutory changes, for the most part, in the latter half of the nineteenth century. Ancient religions did not bar abortion, and neither did Greek and Roman law. At common law, abortion was never established as a crime.

Even after *Roe v. Wade,* abortions remain a hot button emotional issue in this country. The morality and legality of abortions raises a number of emotion-packed questions still debated. It is generally conceded that an <u>unfertilized</u> ovum is not a human being because every time a woman ovulates and fails to become impregnated, at least one ovum dies if it is not fertilized and it is then excreted from her body during menstruation. If it were a human being, the bizarre conclusion would have to be that her failure to get herself impregnated every time she ovulates would be negligent homicide. The thought, of course, is preposterous.

Another question is whether or not a <u>fertilized</u> egg is a human being. Beginning with Pythagoras in ancient Greece and continuing today among various religions, the egg is considered to be animate from the moment of conception. This position is based on the belief that life is created when the ovum is fertilized. Others argue that life, like any other form of energy, can be neither created nor destroyed. Since the egg and the sperm were both alive *before* the egg was fertilized, the vested life energy in both the egg and the sperm is simply *re-vested* into a single living organism, and no new life is created

However, if the fertilized ovum is a human being, a conclusion almost as bizarre as the preceding one must be drawn. Suppose the ovum were successfully fertilized *in vitro*. Suppose further that the doctor or attending technician negligently failed to place the Petri dish containing the fertilized ovum in the incubator overnight and, consequently, it died. Would the doctor or attending technician be guilty of negligent homicide?

Another popular view is that the fetus becomes a human being when it first begins to move. This is said to occur sometime between 24 and 28 weeks after conception. It is then said to be viable; that is, it is capable of living outside the mother's body. Although the fetus might live, having thus been born 10 or 11 weeks prematurely, the chances of it growing into a producing adult would not be good.

There is also the question that, if the fertilized ovum is a human being, would killing it be justifiable homicide? In other words, would an abortion be the taking of a human life as a matter of right in furtherance of the goals of society the same as shooting to death an enemy soldier or executing a convicted murderer? There is a strong argument that society does not have a goal anymore for increasing the size of the population. The population of the world is now too large, and the ratio of producers to eaters in the United States is much too small and likely to become smaller over time. The goal must be to either to reduce the size of the population or to hold it steady and to improve the producer/eater ratio. Abortions can be a useful means for accomplishing those goals.

We have also seen it argued that, except for certain circumstances enumerated above, the killing of a human being is wrong because it leads to feuding, and society cannot tolerate feuding. Would killing (aborting) the fertilized ovum in its various stages of its development lead to feuding in society? One never hears of a feud being started because of such a killing. Who would start it?

Next comes the question of ownership. Do the *unfertilized* eggs in a woman's ovaries belong to her? Does she own them? She must, just as she owns her liver, her hands, or her kidneys. After all, they are all parts of her body. Who else would own them? The next question is, does a *fertilized* egg in her womb belong to her? Does she own it? Well, if it is a human being, perhaps, the answer is that nobody owns it. However, a case can be made that she still owns it the same as she did before it was fertilized. If she owns it *and* if it is a human being, it would be a slave (one human being owned by another), and the mother would be a slaver. That would be illegal and, again, preposterous.

If she owns it and it is not a human being, does she have the right to kill it or to have it killed? It has been argued above that the killing of any organism other than a human being is morally and legally permissible, so long as the killer owns the organism (or has permission from the owner to kill it) and so long as the killing is not done wantonly or cruelly.

These questions and more were answered by *Roe v. Wade,* which decided that the fetus was not an human being with constitutional rights, and that a right to privacy inherent in the Fourteenth Amendment's due process guarantee of personal liberty protected a woman's decision to have an abortion. During the first trimester of pregnancy, the Court held the decision should be left entirely to a woman and her doctor. The Court allowed for some regulation of abortion procedures in the second trimester and some restriction of abortion in the third, in recognition of the legitimate interest that States have in protecting both the pregnant woman's health and the potentiality of human life.

B. Birthed Feticide.

Society needs to go beyond *Roe v. Wade,* extending the period during which a fetus can be put to death beyond its issuance from the mother's body. Today, when the fetus issues from the mother's body, it is considered by everybody to be a human being with all of the rights thereof, and the killing of a human being is both illegal and immoral. It is homicide. The law needs to provide that a birthed fetus does not assume the status of a human being until two events take place: it breathes, and it suckles. Newborns must breathe, assisted or unassisted, shortly after they issue from the mother's body or they will die, but they do not and cannot suckle until they are presented with the nipple. The presentation can be delayed for hours. Until both of these events take place, the fetus cannot exist outside of the mother's body, and the law should consider it to be a birthed fetus and not a human being. Having issued from the mother's body is not enough. The law should also be changed to provide that, when the birth to unmarried or to welfare parents is discovered, the parents lose all legal right to the newborn.

In Chapter 5, Section E, the question is asked, what would happen if there was not available a pre-approved couple willing and able to adopt the newborn? The answer is that, as a last resort, the best thing to do would be to put the birthed fetus to death – send it back through the curtain to wherever it was that it came from. Place it in a plastic bag and seal the bag. The newborn would suffocate to death in a few minutes. It would be quick and painless and save the birthed fetus a lifetime of probable unhappiness, and society the expense of wholly or partially supporting the child until it reached adulthood – and perhaps beyond.

If a fetus were born to parents married or unmarried with a serious defect (condition, abnormality, or disease) not correctable at all or correctable only at great expense, then it should be put to death by suffocation the same as a child born out of wedlock without ready, willing, able, and available adoptive parents. Newborns grossly underweight, or birthed by a mother with HIV, or who is on drugs, is an alcoholic or a heavy smoker should be included in the same category with and treated in the same way as those newborns with uncorrectable birth defects. There are two dozen or more such defects which can be identified by doctors with a cursory postnatal examination. These birthed fetuses are allowed to live only at great cost to society which usually has to provide in whole or in part for their special care during their entire lives, and they can rarely lead normal lives. Parents, in an effort to compensate for the defect, frequently allocate a disproportionate amount of their resources to such a child to the detriment of their other children. Schools also are required under the Americans with Disabilities Act to devote a disproportionate amount of their resources to such children to the detriment of their other pupils. Considering the cost of letting such newborns live and the often unhappy lives that they lead, it is better to humanely terminate their lives right after the postnatal examination during which the defect is detected and before the birthed fetus is allowed access to the nipple. Here again, some may consider this to be a heartless thing to do, but it is best for everyone. Owners of pets would do the same for them in a heartbeat.

Fetuses born outside a hospital with serious defects, or born to unmarried parents, or born to married parents on welfare, without knowledge of local government authorities, and allowed to breathe and suckle would become human beings with all of the rights of human beings. Such children would, of course, be allowed to live and would be put up by the state for adoption if – in the case of unmarried parents – they would not agree to marry or could not qualify for a marriage license. If these arrangements did not work out, government would place the child in a state-supported boarding school and provide for it during its lifetime up to adulthood. Mothers who wilfully concealed the birth of a child under such circumstances would be required to submit to sterilization in order to prevent a recurrence of such an event in the future. Fathers complicit in the wilful concealment would also be required to submit to sterilization.

Occasionally, one reads about a young unmarried woman (who has managed somehow to conceal her pregnancy) going out with a date to a dance, giving birth in a public restroom, allowing the child to die or aiding in its death, cleaning herself up and going back to the dance. Or a young girl giving birth in the bathroom of the family home before school, tossing the fetus down the garbage chute, and then continuing on to school. When the fetus dies, such young mothers are sometimes prosecuted for murder. This is tragic and should never happen. These young mothers have done something of the right thing. It would be better if the newborn were put up for adoption, but young women in this circumstance have no way of arranging that. They know that they have no way of supporting the child, and it would not have a chance of leading a normal, happy life. It is better for all concerned – the newborn, the mother, and society at large – that the life be terminated at birth. Such prosecutions would not happen if the newborn were not considered to be a human being until it had issued from the mother's body <u>and</u> both breathed and suckled.

C. Suicide and Assisted Suicide.

Taking one's own life voluntarily and intentionally is suicide (self-inflicted homicide). Religion holds that life is a gift from God and when infused into the body of a human being is not to be removed either by that person or any other person. Exceptions are made, of course, for taking someone else's life for reasons such as self-defense, executions decreed by law, and military action. Are there pragmatic reasons why religion and government consider suicide to be immoral and illegal? Consider teenagers who have a relatively high suicide rate. Parents – and, to some extent, society at large – expend a great deal of time and

187

effort in raising their children up to their teen years, when they are close to becoming adult producers. It seems a shame to waste all of that time and effort by the teenager committing suicide, especially when he has the potential for some day becoming a producer and even (possibly) helping the parents. Society needs these potential producers as well, not only for what they will be able to contribute to society in peacetime, but also to serve in the armed forces during time of war. Thus, both parents and society at large have an interest in discouraging teenage suicide. Hence, religions and governments have mores and laws prohibiting it. For parents, there is an even more compelling argument against their committing suicide. If parents take their own lives, society at large will have to raise the children. Society does not want this burden.

What are the arguments for mores and laws against the aged and the infirm committing suicide? These arguments are not strong at all, especially if such persons are being supported by their children or by society at large; that is, if they are unfunded eaters. They are too old to serve in the armed forces. They do not have children to support. The question comes down solely to the sentimental consideration of how they would be missed by their friends and relatives if they were no longer living. Most people believe that doctors and nurses, on occasion, have surreptitiously aided suicides for the aged. Laws criminalizing assisting suicides have been challenged in recent years by Dr. Jack Kevorkian, who was prosecuted several times unsuccessfully, but a jury was finally found willing to convict him for his open role in assisting suicides. Still, these archaic laws remain on the books in all but a few jurisdictions. Why should these laws be on the books in the first place? Lawgivers and religionists have been loath to recognize that many old people wish to die. Although they wish it, they do not have the means to accomplish their wish, especially when they are warehoused in a prison or nursing home or even in an assisted living home.

If an older person is suffering severe pain without letup and with no possibility of relief, or if a person is old and no longer enjoys a quality of life, or if he is simply tired of living, if he does not want to be a continuing burden on his children or on other members of society, why should religion or government care if he takes his own life? Or if someone else assists him in doing so, provided suitable measures are taken to assure that his life is not taken against his wishes? Friends and family may care, but religions and governments should not. Religionists say that life is God-given, and it would be a sacrilege to do anything but live it right down to the bitter end, regardless of conditions. However, there is no practical reason why taking one's own life (save when he is young or has someone else dependent upon him) should it be either illegal or immoral, especially when the goal of society is not to increase or even maintain the size of the population.

A prime way to reduce the number of eaters and improve the ratio of producers to eaters is to provide the legal means for people who are permanently incapable of caring for themselves or who simply do not want to live any longer to painlessly take their own lives when they wish to do so. Nursing homes, assisted living homes and prisons are full of such people.

Not only should local governments legalize suicide and assisted suicide, but they should provide for at least one House of Last Goodbyes in every city. This would be a refuge where a sick or elderly person could go to end his life at government expense painlessly, with dignity and without danger to others, such as by leaping from a building onto the street. Neither a waiting period, completion of a great deal of paperwork, nor fulfilling a lot of legal technicalities would be required. The house would provide private surroundings where a person could receive the last rites in the religion of his choice if he wished. In a pleasant and comfortable environment, he could be given an intravenous anesthetic to put him to sleep followed by an injection of a fatal dose of a barbiturate or other drug that would terminate his life peacefully and painlessly. Further, the HLG would cremate the body and arrange for disposition of the ashes according to the wishes of the deceased. The establishing and operation of such houses would not be without cost, but the cost would be more than offset by the reduction in assisted living and nursing home costs. Existing mortuaries could easily be converted to HLGs. A law should require that nursing homes, assisted living homes, prisons and other such institutions give access to representatives of the HLGs so they can make known to residents the services they offer.

D. Euthanasia.

In the wild animal domain, old, sick, and injured herd animals are simply left behind when they cannot keep up, and are killed by predators or starve to death. Old animals that live in packs or families, such as wolves and lions, are often banished from the pack to shift for themselves, which usually leads to a hastened demise. It is natural. Primitive societies do the same thing. Eskimos, even those who were the best hunters in their prime, receive the poorest cuts from the kills when they are old and can no longer hunt. Poor nutrition takes its toll. Nomadic tribes simply leave the infirm behind when they can no longer keep up, only to die from thirst, starvation, or from attacks by predators. What else can such societies do? However, in most so-called "advanced" civilizations, the aged and infirm are revered and cared for until they die of natural causes, regardless of how long that takes, how much it costs, or how much they suffer. The medical arts have made remarkable strides in devising treatments and procedures to extend our lives. Senior citizens are often healthy and lead satisfying lives by reason of the availability of medical regimes, but not always. Medical achievements sometimes extend a person's life, but the quality of the extended life is poor. Who among us wants to sit around in a nursing home watching TV all day and being fed oatmeal at meal time by an attendant who scrapes the excess off his chin with the spoon? What kind of a life is that?

When aged and infirm human beings who are not contributing to society and have no responsibility to society – eaters – drift into this predicament, those with money may use their own resources to pay for their keep. These are funded eaters. Those who are indigent –unfunded eaters – may be eligible for Medicaid, which pays for the care of the indigent, sick, and disabled in nursing homes and assisted living homes, or for Supplemental Security Income which provides income for the sick and disabled of all ages. All eaters may have other options: One may be for their own children or other relatives to take care of them either by themselves or by paying the fees for their care in nursing or assisted living homes. Another option would be charities that might be willing to assume the burden. Absent the availability of any of these options, unfunded eaters have no alternative but to live in the streets, sleeping in doorways or under bridges, eating out of dumpsters and surviving however they can. They ought to have another option which should be to voluntarily and easily choose the services of a House of Last Goodbyes.

The services of an HLG should also be available, with close controls, for next-of-kin to exercise for their elderly relatives who have advanced Alzheimer's disease or other severe impairment that completely deprives them permanently of their cognitive capabilities. Such people do not know where they are, who they are, or who anyone else is, including their own children. Life for them is over, though they are not yet clinically dead; they are a total burden on society. Such an option sounds cruel and callous at first glance, but it really isn't. Consider that we do this all the time for beloved pets that are sick, old, and infirm. Allowing people to continue in such a dreadful state is what is really inhumane.

Think of this parallel situation: A person is severely brain damaged in an automobile accident but is alive when entering the hospital and is there placed on a life support system. Doctors say he could not live without the life support system and will never recover. The patient is brain dead but not clinically dead. Under such circumstances today, next-of-kin may allow the patient to die by pulling the plug on the life support system without fear of prosecution by the state. What is so different about pulling the plug on an advanced Alzheimer's patient?

Moral codes are created and laws enacted by people (not by God through the church as many would have us believe) for the express purpose of protecting and furthering the ends and needs of society. A society's moral code and its laws should always be in harmony. When the ends and needs of society change, then changes also need to be made in the moral code and in the law. Therefore, the relationship between society's ends and needs on the one hand and the moral code and law on the other needs to be reviewed as an ongoing process because the events, circumstances, and conditions that affect society are constantly changing. Society and its institutions have to be alert to these changes and to act or react accordingly.

Part III. The Electoral System

Chapter 12. The Current Electoral System.

For thousands of years, the people of the world have had important decisions affecting their lives made by a few other people – by leaders. Leaders became leaders through heredity, military force, or through some religious or political process. The people in the United States are fortunate to live in a democracy where we are privileged to select our own leaders. Unfortunately, our system for selecting leaders, our electoral system, is badly flawed and needs to be replaced. Because, even in a hotly contested presidential election, less than 50 percent of the registered voters bother going to the polls, voters are commonly thought to be uncaring or apathetic about politics and government. However, voter inactivity is more probably due to voters correctly perceiving that they have nothing to say about the initial selection of candidates for political office at the federal, state or local level. In primaries, they have to vote for someone on a slate of candidates that they had no role in selecting.

It is inarguable that no candidate in presidential elections, congressional, state, and local government elections has much of a chance of winning unless he is endorsed by the leaders of the Democratic or Republican party. Candidates who may run in the primaries on the party ticket are selected by the leaders of these two parties at all three levels of government. Party leaders themselves were not elected to these positions. They got into those leadership positions in some other way. Of the candidates thus "anointed" by party leaders, the winner of the primary election is then at liberty to run in the general election that follows. Political conventions and caucuses are the same. The candidate, thus elected, is obligated to the party leaders when he takes office both for allowing him on the party's ticket in the first place and for the party's support during the general election that follows

This flaw permeates the nation's political system at every level, including levels below local government. Candidates for the officers of Parent-Teachers Associations, local civic associations, condominium associations, and the like are usually selected by nominating committee members, who are appointed by a president or chairman of the association. The committee members sound out those individuals in the organization with whom they are acquainted and whom they feel would be good officers of the association. Then, at an annual meeting of the association, the membership gets to vote on the slate of candidates selected by the committee. As a nod to democracy, members are permitted to nominate candidates from the floor at the annual meeting, but rarely is one nominated because everyone knows they would have little chance of being elected. So, the "election of officers" as it is called is actually a ratification by the membership of the slate of candidates selected by the nominating committee who are, in turn, selected by the president or chairman. Members vote for the slate because there is nothing else to do and, in doing so, often feel like a rubber stamp – which is what they are. Reduced to the role of a rubber stamp, most potential voters understandably take little or no interest in the so-called election process.

This same flaw afflicts industry's electoral system as well. The policy-making and operations-review organization in industry is the board of directors. Theoretically, members of the board of directors should be both nominated and elected by the stockholders. Unfortunately, it often does not work quite that way because, while large stockholders have some limited capability for nominating board members, small stockholders have no way at all. Consequently, board members are often nominated by the chief executive officer. When such nominees are elected (read *ratified*) by the stockholders, the board itself becomes, in effect, a rubber stamp for whatever course the CEO wishes to take. In light of the many corporate scandals that came to light in the year 2002, and in accordance with the Sarbanes-Oxley corporate governance legislation, many corporations are taking action to make their boards more independent of management.

A second flaw in our current electoral system is that candidates become obligated, not only to party leaders, but to their campaign contributors as well. Political campaigns, as they are now constituted, are expensive, long, drawn-out, and often assume a carnival atmosphere ill-suited to the importance of the task at hand. Only those candidates who are personally very wealthy or who are able to command wealth can run. When candidates do not have personal wealth they are able to command it by tacitly agreeing in advance that, once elected, they will take positions on issues favorable to the those who have contributed to their campaigns. Candidates like to euphemize that they agree to allow the contributors " access" to them personally to make their cases for whatever it is the contributors want. What the contributors will want is favorable tax treatment, a protective tariff, price supports and the like, all of which will cost ordinary taxpayers in the form of either higher taxes, higher prices or both. Thus, going into the general election, candidates are burdened with obligations to their campaign contributors as well as to their party leaders.

A third flaw as mentioned in the previous paragraph is that the current electoral system is very expensive and very inefficient to operate. Considering the cost of travel for federal, state, and local campaigners and their staffs all over the country, television and radio advertising costs, the cost of printing brochures, banners and signs, not to mention the time spent by the candidates and their staffs, must cause any thinking person to wonder if the same result cannot be accomplished in a vastly cheaper way. The nation could well use the money spent on these campaigns for other more worthy purposes.

Chapter 13. The Grass Roots Empowerment Electoral System.

It has become possible for the individual citizen to be much more closely involved in the political process than ever before. A great preponderance of the people in the United States are literate, if not in English then in their native tongue. Radio and television provide nearly real-time access to major current events so that listeners and viewers are in about as good of a position to know about and make their own decisions with respect to current events and issues as are leaders. Although there are people who have little or no interest in current events, millions do, as evidenced by writers of letters to editors, by callers on radio talk shows, and by callers to their legislators.

The Grass Roots Empowerment Electoral System (GREES) proposed here rests on the premise that the electoral system in a true democracy must begin with the individual registered voter. The GREES objective is to base political power with the individual voter right at the beginning and at the grass roots, to insure that the voters' views and wishes are reflected upward through the political hierarchy on a continuing basis and to insure that information and questions on issues are routinely cascaded down through the system to them for consideration, reflection, and action. The voters must be in control. Now they are really not. Special interest groups, politicians and the media are. Changes in the electoral system can be commenced immediately without waiting for political, social, or economic changes. Changes in political organizations and the electoral system, prompted by economic changes, will be needed eventually but not at the outset.

There is nothing novel about the GREES concept. The president and the vice president of the United States are elected by the Electoral College. Electors themselves are either appointed at state party conventions or the names of electors appear on state ballots. After being appointed or elected, the electors from the 50 states meet in closed session and customarily vote for their party's nominees for president and vice president of the United States, although they are not required by the Constitution to do so. Also, until 1913 when the Seventeenth Amendment to the Constitution of the United States was ratified, senators to the United States Congress were elected by state legislatures, an arrangement analogous to the one proposed here. As another example of elections similar to the one proposed here, cardinals in the Roman Catholic Church elect the pope this way in a closed session.

1. Advantages of the GREES.

First, the GREES would easily overcome the single greatest fault of the current electoral system, which is that the initial selection of government officials rests elsewhere than with the voters. It is overcome because, in the final configuration of GREES, there are no nominations. Candidates are only elected from slates of candidates that have themselves been elected beginning with the individual voter selecting his block captain. Block captains elect their neighborhood chairman. Neighborhood chairmen elect their precinct chairman. In larger local government units, the level of ward would be in the electoral hierarchy and so on up the hierarchy to the very top.

GREES would also easily overcome the second and third faults of the current electoral system; namely, that the current electoral system is expensive, and candidates have to solicit campaign funds from political blocs and special interest groups to finance their campaigns, obligating themselves in the process. GREES would be cheap to operate. The only costs would be for transportation and per diem expenses while electors were sequestered in a closed session to elect electors or candidates. The little money needed to defray the expenses of the election meetings at local, state, and national levels would be furnished from the funds of those political entities. Candidates would not have to obligate themselves to acquire campaign funds. Incumbents at each political level would be responsive only to the majority of their constituents and to nobody else.

Any citizen could be elected as president of the United States, although the competition along the way would surely be fierce. As a practical matter, many of our present incumbents would be reelected up through the political hierarchy because of their political skills, but they would have to start at the bottom in every election. The number of full-time career politicians would be greatly diminished. Most elected politicians would need a day job.

There would be additional advantages. Opinion polls would no longer be needed. Information and questions on many issues would be cascaded downward through this organization by means of the Internet, e-mail, postal mail and telephone. Citizens would not be as dependent upon the media for information as they now are, and the media would lose much of its capacity for molding public opinion. Lobbyists would be out of busiiness. Political parties may gradually become useless in this environment. Expensive and circus-like party conventions would be passé. The ubiquitous signs and billboards cluttering up the landscape to advertise candidates would disappear. Radio and television would no longer be glutted with expensive political advertisements.

2. Implementing GREES

Enormous obstacles will have to be overcome to implement the GREES. Three requirements must be fulfilled in order for it to work: First, information about GREES must be disseminated widely throughout the United States. Exactly how this can be accomplished is uncertain. Indeed, *whether* it can be accomplished is uncertain. Second, there will be massive resistance from politicians and political parties, special interest groups and the media that would have to be overcome. They would resist because they would all have much to lose. Third, a large majority of adults must be persuaded of the system's merits enough to want to give it a try; that is, they must be convinced that it will be better than the system we have now. In other words they must be convinced that the devil they don't know would be better than the devil they do know. Fortunately, GREES can be, should be, and needs to be tried first at the local level. People can see how it works at local levels before deciding whether or not to try it at the state and national levels.

a. Meetings.

All GREES elections would be conducted in meetings. There would be no more going to the polls, no more hanging chads. There would be no more political conventions, primaries, caucuses or general elections. The GREES in its final configuration would replace the present electoral system in its entirety. Meetings for electing officials would be limited to members of the voting group only and closed to others. For example, only individual voters would attend their block meetings. Only block captains would attend neighborhood meetings, and so on. Meetings below the local level (i.e., below the town, city, county, or parish level) would be held once a year in a residence or a room of a local school, church, or a hotel meeting room for larger groups. Such meetings would not normally require more than a few hours and certainly no longer than a day or two. Minutes for these meetings would be taken by a secretary elected by the group. After the minutes were approved by the group, they would be disseminated to the constituency.

Meetings for election of officials at the local government level and above would be on even years. Meetings for state and national government officials would be every other even (fourth) year. Members of the voting group at the local government level and above would be sequestered in a section of a hotel with no member being allowed to communicate with anyone outside the meeting or to leave the meeting (emergencies excepted) until the voting of the group was completed. A member, having left, would not be allowed to return. The only other individuals allowed in the section would be service and security personnel. The voting might conceivably take a week or two before it was completed. A limit would be set on the length of the meetings. A group unable to elect an elector during the given time period for its meeting would forgo representation at higher levels of government until the next election. Incumbent officers would continue to serve until new ones were elected. Minutes would be taken by a public secretarial service and disseminated after approval by the group.

  b. Voting.

Candidates would always be selected from within the group doing the voting. For example, neighborhood chairmen would only be elected from among the block captains in the neighborhood. Winners would be decided by majority vote. Votes would be proportional to the number of constituents each voter had. The member of the group with the smallest number of voters in his constituency would have one vote and the other members would have proportionately more, rounded to the nearest whole number. Local, state and national government councils would always have an odd number of members, preferably less than the arbitrary number of 10, to better assure a majority and to keep councils from becoming unwieldy. Boards should have 50 or less.

  c. Duties.

The regular duties of the block captain would be to remain in fairly close communication with the members of the block. He would need to be aware of people moving into and moving out of his block, welcome them in, see them out, and report the information to the chairman of his neighborhood. He would provide block members with information about current issues received from above in the GREES hierarchy; obtain their views on issues, local, state, and federal, communicate the essence of their views upward to the chairman of the neighborhood, and intercede with government on behalf of block members. He would also be responsible for keeping a running count of those in his block, including registered voters, and for insuring that eligible residents had taken steps to be qualified voters. The counts of block captains would ultimately become the basis for the United States census as these counts were aggregated upward through the states to the federal government. Thus, the U.S. Census would be continuing and always updated. Instead of the Bureau of Census gearing up to a herculean effort for a once-every-ten-years census, the Bureau would engage in continually processing data, and auditing and spot-checking group, district, ward, city, and state head counts on a regular basis. State and federal census bureaus would also have responsibility for punishing intentional miscounting and misreporting.

The sole duty of vice block captains and all other "vice" officials in the GREES would be to act for the principal official in his absence and possibly assist him in his duties. The sole duty of the block secretary and all other secretaries would be to take and keep minutes of meetings. The duties of treasurers would be to take up collections at the block meeting, make payments for the block as required and keep a record of receipts and disbursements. Contributions to the collection would be entirely voluntary, as would the amounts contributed. All adult residents of the block would be welcome as members, whether or not they contributed to the collection. The neighborhood, precinct and ward chairmen would be responsible for: receiving information and questions from above in the GREES hierarchy and disseminating them to block captains within the neighborhood; gathering information from block captains on the views of their block members on specific subjects; consolidating these into the views or positions of the neighborhood; passing them upward; and representing his neighborhood where needed. Duties would be the same for officials at other levels of the hierarchy below the local government level. The duties of local, state and national government officials would remain much the same as they are now.

    d. Steps for Implementing of GREES.

    Any adult citizen can start implementing the GREES where he lives. The first step would be to identify 10 or more homes in his immediate neighborhood as a block. Considerable flexibility is needed to do this because of varying geographical situations and the means of communication available to residents. If homes are close together, it may be feasible to have more voters in the group than if they are spread out. In an apartment building, a block might be apartments on one or more floors; in an urban or suburban community, a block might be the homes on a street or streets; in a rural community, blocks might be by area. Ideally, much of the communication would be by e-mail, telefax, or Internet web sites. If all or most of the residents have computers, the communication problem will be vastly reduced, so the group can be larger. Otherwise, communication would be by whatever means were available, including telephone, audio and video cassettes, newsletters, regular mail, hand bills, and personal visits.

    The second step would be to talk to the neighbors in the block about GREES. Try to persuade them to form a GREES block. Having formed a block, try to get block members together to elect block officers. Try to identify someone in the neighborhood who appears to have the qualities that you consider appropriate for a public official. Try to persuade him to stand for election as block captain. Either that, or you might consider standing for election as block captain yourself, or as one of the other three officers. If you are elected as block captain, try to get yourself elected for a position at the neighborhood level and for positions as high up in the GREES hierarchy as he want to go. If a person does not wish to be active, at least he should attend the block meeting once every year to elect officers, ask questions, discuss and vote.

The third step would be taken by the block captain once elected. It would be to get a street or area map of the area where he lives. Usually, the city or county government will have a map of the city or county, the appropriate section of which can be blown up on a copier. Or one can find such a map on the Internet. Next, he should select an area that includes his block and has readily identified boundaries, such as roads, streets, streams, ridges, or buildings. This would be the neighborhood. Here again, flexibility in size must be a consideration, but a neighborhood of perhaps 200 to 500 houses or apartments might be about the right size. It would be handy if a church or a school could be included because they may provide an occasional meeting place. Then the block captain should divide the neighborhood around his block into what he thinks would be other appropriately-sized blocks. (These may well have to be adjusted later.)

Fourth, with the help of other members of his block, the block captain should draft a handbill giving his name, postal address, telephone number, e-mail address, and fax number. Explain what he has already done and his purpose for sending the handbill. Attach a copy of the map, make copies of the handbill and hand-distribute them to each house or apartment in the neighborhood area. Request information about the household, including number of adults, registered voters, children, the postal address, telephone number, e-mail address, and telefax address. Promise privacy of the information. Conclude by asking members of each block identified on the map to assemble themselves at a stated time and place for the purpose of electing a block captain, vice captain, treasurer, and secretary, and then let the initiating block captain know when they have done it. Candidates would be those who have volunteered. If nobody volunteered, the block captain and members of his block would make personal visits in an effort to recruit volunteers.

As the fifth step, after enough blocks in the neighborhood had their elections, the block captains would meet for the purpose of electing a neighborhood chairman, vice chairman, secretary, and treasurer. The neighborhood chairman would also serve as the elector to the next higher level in the political hierarchy–probably the precinct. The block captains would continue as the neighborhood's board of directors and would meet perhaps once or twice a year to cope with any problems raised by the chairman as requiring their attention.

The sixth step, after the neighborhood board has been organized and officers elected, would be for the board to turn its attention to tentatively identifying other neighborhoods abutting their own. For example, if the newly-formed neighborhood were in the seventh precinct of a city, the board would identify other potential neighborhoods abutting their own in the seventh precinct. Then the chairman would assign block captains, as individual members of his neighborhood board, to contact individuals in those neighborhoods to try to interest them in forming a GREES neighborhood similar to their own.

Seven, the neighborhood chairman, as the neighborhood elector, would meet with other neighborhood electors to elect precinct officers. Those neighborhood electors collectively would continue to serve as the GREES's precinct board of directors and would continue to hold their positions as neighborhood chairmen. This process would be repeated for other precincts. In larger cities, there might be yet another level (ward) in the political heirarchy. If a city were not in a county or parish, the precinct chairmen, as electors, would constitute the GREES local government board of directors. If a city were a political entity within a county, an elector chosen by the city board of directors, along with electors from other political entities within the county, would also constitute a GREES county government board of directors.

e. Phases of the GREES

In Phase I, the GREES local government board of directors would elect from within their own number GREES candidates for city, county, or parish council. These candidates would have to timely qualify and run as a slate of GREES candidates in accordance with the existing electoral system as currently prescribed by the local government charter. The difference would be that the views and goals of the GREES would be distilled upward from the bottom beginning with the individual voter, instead of being handed down from the top.

In Phase II, once a majority of council members had been elected as GREES candidates in accordance with the existing electoral system, the local government council would then proceed to request the state legislature to revise the election rules for that local government unit to allow the GREES local government board of directors every two years to elect council members, an executive (chairman, mayor, burgess etc.) and (every other even year) a state elector directly without holding a general election. To obtain such permission from the state government, it surely would have to be shown that the GREES represented the majority of the voters in the local government unit and that all voters in the local government unit were eligible to be members of the GREES if they chose to be. After the charter had been revised, the local government board of directors would meet on even years to elect local government council members, an executive and (every other even year) a state elector.

This same process would be extended upward to state legislatures and to the Congress. Initially, in Phase I, GREES local government electors meeting every other even year (every fourth year) as the state board of directors would elect and field as many GREES candidates for governor, state delegate and senator positions up for election as they could. Only in Phase II, after the state constitution had been changed, would these electors, meeting as the state board of directors (replacing the state legislature), elect the members of the state executive council, a governor, and a national elector.

In Phase I, the 50 national electors meeting as the national board of directors would nominate GREES candidates to run for president and positions in Congress. It would be only in Phase II after the U.S. Constitution had been changed revising the national election system that national GREES electors from all 50 states, meeting as the national board of directors (replacing the Congress), in the same fourth year that state officials were elected, elect a national council and a president of the United States.

Thus, the individual voter would have a say, directly or indirectly, about who was elected for every political position that concerned him. Any block captain could be elected as President of the United States, although the competition along the way would surely be fierce. As a practical matter, many of our present incumbent politicians would be reelected up through the GREES political hierarchy because of their political skills, but they would all have to start at the bottom and would all be obligated only to their constituents.

During the initial phase of GREES, the schedule would be that dictated by the local, state and national rules and laws. During the second phase, elections would be at twelve levels, and the schedule for elections might look like this:

No.	Positions	Periods	Freq.
1	Block Officers	1st full wk in Jan	Ann.
2	Neighborhood Officers	3rd full wk in Jan	Ann.
3	Precinct Officers	1st full wk in Feb	Ann.
4	Ward Officers	3rd full wk in Feb	Ann.
5	Town or City Bd Members	1st full wk in March	Even Yrs
6	Town or City Council Members, CEO, and Elector	1st full wk in April	Even yrs
7	County or Parish Bd Members	Last wk in April & 1st wk in May	Even yrs
8	County or Parish Council Members, CEO, and Elector	Last wk in May & 1st wk in June	Even yrs
9	State Board Members	1st & 2nd full wks in Sep	*

10	State Council Members, CEO (Gov) and Elector	1st & 2nd full wks in Oct	*
11	National Bd Members	1st & 2nd full wks in Nov	*
12	National Council & CEO (President)	2nd & 3rd full wks in Dec	*

* Every other even year, coinciding with the years during which the President is currently elected

About the Author

The author, BA, MBA, JD and member of the Virginia Bar, worked for the federal government in administrative and management capacities for 40 years. For the last 25 of those 40 years, he was associate director for a government bureau in Washington, D.C. It was from this position that he observed the workings of the federal government up close.